*In the Name of Allah, the Beneficent, the Merciful*

# THE HISTORY OF

# ISLAM AND BLACK NATIONALISM

# IN THE AMERICAS

Adib Rashad
(James Miller)

Writers' Inc.
Beltsville, Maryland

Library of Congress Catalog Card Number: 91-65222
ISBN 0-9627854-1-5

First printed in the United States of America 1985.
Registration Number TXu 193-266

Second edition 1991.

Cover: The cover of this book is a reproduction of an original work by Mary Greer Mudiku, a noted Washington, D.C. artist. The figures are: (left to right) Top row: Elijah Muhammad; Marcus Garvey. Second row: W.D. Muhammad; Noble Drew Ali; Malcolm X. Third row: Ibrahima (Abdul Rahman); Louis Farrakhan.

Writers' Inc. publishes literary works of value to the spiritual, economic and scientific development of individuals and communities. Please write us for additional information:

Writers' Inc.
P.O. Box 746
Beltsville, Maryland 20705

# CONTENTS

# To The Reader

---

This book is an exploratory anthology that I observed was missing in the continuing development of African American History. Hopefully, I, along with others, will extend and expand this historically neglected subject.

I should also add that since the initial writing of this book five years ago, a lot has happened with regard to the African American Muslim community (Umma). For instance, Imam Warith Dean Muhammad and Minister Louis Farrakhan have contradicted some of my earlier statements regarding their leadership roles. Furthermore, a national Islamic organization, The National Islamic Assembly (NIA) has been established for the purpose of organizing African American Muslims on a non-sectarian basis.

Insha Allah, the onward progress of African American Muslims in particular, and African Americans in general will continue.

# Dedication

---

**I** dedicate this book to all freedom loving people in the world. I make a special dedication to Marcus Mosiah Garvey, Nobel Drew Ali, and Elijah Muhammad. May Allah be Pleased with their good intentions and forgive them for their mistakes.

# Acknowledgments

I extend my heartfelt thanks and appreciation to the special people who gave me the incentive to complete this project. I extend profound thanks to Dr. Muhammad El-Khawas of the University of the District of Columbia, who inspired the idea for this project. I am also grateful for his professional assistance. I extend my warmest thanks to Dr. William McDonald, also of the University of the District of Columbia for his much needed assistance in the area of proofreading, and his intellectual advice.

Special thanks and appreciation is given to Oduno Tarik of the Universal Negro Improvement Association (UNIA), and Dr. Sulayman S. Nyang of Howard University for their selfless assistance in the area of research and organization of certain material. Dr. Nyang was extremely encouraging. Heartfelt thanks is extended to Dora E. Murray-Tolliver for her constant encouragement and confidence in my efforts. I also extend my deepest thanks to Ms. Cheryl D. Lane (now, Aimira Rashad) for her assistance in xeroxing and her perceptive critiques. I am extremely grateful for the existence of the Schomburg Research Center in New York, the Moreland Spingarn Research Library at Howard University and the Library of Congress.

I give sentimental thanks and appreciation to the Honorable Elijah Muhammad for his tireless efforts intrying to uplift this fallen piece of Black humanity. May Allah bless his deeds and memory. I also thank Imam Warith Deen Muhammad for carrying the word of Allah and His religion of peace into the annals of contemporary history.

Above all I thank Allah.

The errors or flaws in this project are mine, the compliments or praise belong to Allah. I would be remiss by not thanking Professor Farid I. Muhammad of East-West University in Chicago for taking the bold initiative to include this text in his curriculum, and as a part of his book titled *Education For Self-Reliance.*

# Foreword

The arrival of Islam in the United States of America has been dated back to the coming of slaves from Africa. During this unfortunate trade in human cargo from the African mainland, any Muslim men and women came to these shores. Some of these men and women were more visible than others; some were more literate in Arabic than the others; and some were better remembered by their generations than others. Yet, given these multiple differences between the Muslim slaves and their brethren from various parts of the African continent, the fact still remains that their Islam and their self confidence did not save them from the oppressive chains of slave masters. The religion of Islam survived only during the lifetime of individual believers who tried desperately to maintain their Islamic way of life. Among the Muslims who came into *anti bellum* times in America one can include Yorro Mahmud (erroneously anglicised as Yarrow Mamout), Ayub Ibn Sulayman Diallo (known to Anglo-Saxons as Job ben Solomon), Abdul Rahman (known as Abdul Rahahman in the Western sources) and countless others whose Islamic ritual practices were prevented from surfacing in public.

Besides these Muslim slaves of the *ante bellum* America, there were others who came to these shores without the handicap of slavery. They came from Southern Europe, the Middle East and the Indian Subcontinent. These Muslims were immigrants to America at the end of the Nineteenth Century and the beginning of the Twentieth Century. Motivated by the desire to come to a land of opportunity and strike it rich, many of these men and women later found out that the United States was destined to be their permanent homeland. In their search for identity and cultural security in their environment, these Muslim immigrants began to consolidate their cultural resources by building mosques and organizing national and local groups for the purpose of social welfare and solidarity. These developments among the Muslims contributed to the emergence of various cultural and religious bodies among the America Muslims.

In the drive for self-preservation and cultural integrity these Muslim immigrants encountered many problems. There were problems relating to the maintenance of houses of prayer and to the organization of serious men and women dedicated to the upholding of the tradition of the ancestors from the Old World. There were problems relating to assimilation into the American culture and to the selection of mates by Muslim men whose choice of importing a bride from the homeland had almost vanished because of circumstances in the United States of America. Yet, having said all these about the difficulties of the immigrants from the denying the historical precedence of the African Muslim of *ante bellum* America, Islam became a reality in American society only after the Muslim immigrants of the Twentieth Century began to exercise their freedom of worship in an America where each and every citizen strongly believes in his right to worship differently. Indeed it was this rendezvous between the followers of Islam and the American destiny that facilitated the gradual planting of the Islamic faith in American soil.

The preaching and planting of Islam have not been identified with only the first and second groups of Muslims. This is because of the fact that a third group of Muslims is now inextricably linked to American history

Muslims. This is because of the fact that a third group of Muslims is now inextricably linked to American history and American Society. Who are these Muslims and where do they come from? These are the native born Americans, whites and blacks, who decided to embrace a minority religion in a predominantly Christian country.

Historically speaking, the first native born American Muslim was Muhammad Alexander Russell Webb, a former American consular officer in Manila, Philippines. Prior to his conversion to Islam, Mr. Webb studied extensively the writings of philosophers and sages from the Orient. Islam apparently struck a responsive chord in his soul and he decided to embrace the teachings of the Quran. Writing much later in *Islam in America*, he described his spiritual pilgrimage to Islam and the odds against which he struggled in planting the seed of Islam in America. He started a publication called the *Moslem World* which is indeed the mother of all modern Islamic literature in North America.

The American diplomat's conversion to Islam coincided with the arrival of the Muslim immigrants and it is quite probable the present Islamic movement owed much to the confluence of the immigrant and native efforts at Islamic Dawah. Regardless of what future historians of the Islamic Movement in America will say, the fact remains that Webb's conversion set the precedence for future White Americans to discover and search for the meaning of life in the teachings of the Holy Quran. He also pioneered the Islamic press in America and Muslim editors of our times cannot but recount events relating to this life with admiration and wonderment. He was truly ahead of his time!

But if Mr. Webb was a man of learning and worldwide travels, who found in Islam the spiritual medicine for an American society troubled by the agonies of the receding Victorian Age, many of his contemporaries and successors who then or later encountered Islam or some form of Islamic teachings were not that fortunate in American life. As history would have it, it was Elijah Poole (later renamed Elijah Muhammad) and his Nation of Islam who would see in Islam not the medicine for the salvation of all America but a spiritual and social weapon that could psychologically and emotionally liberate his fellow blacks from the paralyzing grip of racism in American society. To Elijah Muhammad, who was not to be accepted in his lifetime by the mainstream Muslims of the Old World and the New World, Islam was the religion of the Black Man. His teaching of the Nation of Islam was ideologically related somehow to the earlier teachings of Timothy Drew who is now better known as The Prophet Nobel Drew Ali, an African-American who preached to his followers a doctrine that traced the history of blacks back to Morocco and the East. Nobel Drew Ali did not only claim to be a prophet but he established temples around the United States and instructed his followers to add the suffix *bey* after their name. A counterpart to this was the adding of the letter X after the names of the members of the Nation of Islam.

In tracing the history of the development of Islamic ideas in American society, one must point out that two fundamental differences can be discerned between the labors of Mr. Webb on the one hand and the labors of the late Elijah Muhammad on the other. Whereas Mr. Webb was seen as a passing cloud on the American religious horizon, and whereas his movement was never strong enough to justify federal probings of his movement's activities, the late Elijah Muhammad and his Nation of Islam were widely feared as diabolic forces set to destroy American society.    Yet, in identifying the differences between the two postures taken by Mr. Webb and the late Elijah Muhammad, one must hasten to add that the movement of Elijah Muhammad prepared Malcolm X (later renamed Malik Shabazz) to raise the banner of orthodox Islam in America.    Indeed, from the wider perspective of history, one can say that it was in Malcolm X (that is, Malik Shabazz) that history in its game of paradoxes and ironies brought together the two strands of Muslim thought in America.    In Malik Shabazz, there is the unity of thought of the Webbian belief that Islam is the spiritual medicine that could save America from herself and the Elijahian belief that the African-American could only extricate himself by seizing Islam as the antidote to the poison of America anti-Negro racism.

The book of Mr. Adib Rashad (James Miller) is a documentation of the encounter between Islam and the Black peoples of North America.    Working on the assumption that Islam is not a stranger to African-Americans because it was known to many of their ancestors in Africa, Mr. Rashad traced the history of the black American encounter with Islam from the time of slavery to the present. In the course of his investigation and analysis, he identifies the major landmarks in this history. He did not only tell us about the early Muslim slaves of the *ante bellum* period but he also discussed the rise of modern Islam in the cities of America. He showed how colorful historical characters such as Marcus Garvey, Nobel Drew Ali and Farad Muhammad featured in the drama.

Coming to the present period, Mr. Rashad analyses the contemporary situation and the various groups that are now claiming to be the true inheritors and custodians of the Muslim faith in America. He contends that Black Nationalism in North America has been affected by the Islamic Movement and vice versa. He concludes that Islam is now a part of the American social landscape and Muslims must be taken for what they really are. They are part of the United States and their religion is seriously adhered to by almost all members.

In concluding the foreword to this book I would like to draw my readers to three points about the Islamic Movement in North America. First of all, it should be borne in mind that one of the causes for the progress of Islam in the United States lies in her appeal to the lowly and deprived. This is the reason for the Islamic miracle in American prisons. This development is an interesting one, for how many of Webb's generation would have believed that the doctrine he was preaching as a loner in the wilderness would one day be an important source of inspiration and rehabilitation of the society's despised many? Malik Shabazz was a vindication of the Webbian faith in the curative powers of the Islamic faith; and contemporary inmates joining the Islamic fold are potential Malik Shabbazes whose lives could eventually be reconciled to accept the unity of man and the need for the coexistence of the races. The second point that deserves attention here is that Mr. Rashad's study calls for more studies of the Muslim factor in African-American history. This is particularly true for the *ante bellum* period where Muslim slaves were known to be masterminds of rebellion. His study raises many issues that need to be re-examined.

The last point that comes to mind is that the Islamic Movement is now a multiracial, multicultural and multinational force in America.  Not only are Muslims native American converts or descendants of former immigrants, but they are drawn from almost all points on the globe.  The diversity in the Islamic community has created both unity and hopes and aspirations and interpretations and sentiments.  This phenomenon is not particular to the Muslims; it is indeed a part of the American religious reality.  Yet, there is something which is fundamentally unique to the Islamic Movement.  This is the general belief among certain segments of African-America that Islam is the spiritual pillar of their nationalism.  This perhaps is due to the fact that to many African-American intellectuals and students on college campuses, Islam is an African-Asian religion.  As one Third World scholar puts it, Islam is truly a Third World Religion that embraces members from almost all over the Third World.  This is a lesson that one learns from the pages of students such as Mr. Rashad who writes on Islam and the black experiences in the United States.

Sulayman S. Nyang, Ph.D.
Howard University

# The History of Islam in the United States

The historical and controversial period of Islam in the United States begins with the Honorable Nobel Drew Ali (Moorish Scientist), and increases in controversy with the Nation of Islam under the leadership of the Honorable Elijah Muhammad. In these movements Islam became a vehicle by which African-Americans expressed their disdain for a Caucasian majority and their Christian religion; in this, sense black nationalism was subordinate to Islam.

The history of so-called orthodox Islam in America is sketchy and somewhat obscure; however, some worthwhile attempts have been made to place Islam in its rightful historical domain. According to the Encyclopedia of American Religions, the Muslims appeared in the new world of the colonies.

"Istfan the Arab" was a guide to Franciscan explorer Marcos de Niya in Arizona in 1539. Nosereddine, an Egyptian, settled in the Catskills of New York in the 1500's and was burned at the stake for allegedly murdering an Indian princess.

One Arab became a folk hero: Haj Ali, in 1840, was a camel driver for the U.S. Army, and he also experimented with breeding camels in the Arizona desert. He is remembered under his corrupted name, "Hi Jolly".
The Encyclopedia further states that as early as the 1860's, Syrians and Lebanese, fleeing the invading Turks, came to the United States. But the first serious attempt to establish Islam in America followed the conversion of Muhammad Alexander Russell Webb in 1888. Webb was the American

Consul in Manila at the time of his conversion, but returned to New York in 1892. The following year, he opened the Oriental Publishing Company and began a periodical, *The Muslim World*, of which he was the editor. He also wrote a number of booklets. In the same year, he was the only defender of Islamic principles and the faith presented at the Parliament of Religions at Chicago. He died in 1916. [1]

Occurring during the period of Muhammad Russell Webb's conversion and religious activities was the beginning of a large contingent of religious activities was the beginning of a large contingent of immigrants from Eastern Mediterranean -- Syria, Lebanon, Iran, India, Turkey and a number of other Muslim countries. Three thousand Polish Muslims and a small community of Circassian (Russian) Muslims settled in New York. [2] These newly arrived immigrants isolated themselves in clan-like settlements, typical of which was a highly male dominated structure. National and sub-national communities formed in Northern urban centers, particularly in Detroit. According to Dr. Sulayman Nyang, the Arab Muslim immigrants settled along the eastern U.S. seaboard, and in the Mid-West. He states that the first Mosques or Masjids, and Islamic centers were built by Arab settlers in the Mid-West.

---

[1] J Gordon Melton, <u>The Encyclopedia of American Religions</u> (McGrath Publishing Company,Wilmington N.C., 1978), pp. 337 & 338.

[2] <u>Ibid.</u>, pp. 338.

Between 1900 and 1940, Muslim immigration increased considerably. The Muslims from eastern and southern Europe, following the examples of their non-Muslim neighbors, started coming in search of the "American Dream."

These were the Albanians, and the Yugoslav Muslims, who were fleeing from political persecution in their countries, and many of them also settled on the eastern seaboard and the Mid-West.

Nyang continues by stating that besides the two European groups just mentioned, there were Muslims from the Soviet dominated areas, who came from Poland -- they too settled in New York and New Jersey, and carved a place for themselves in the biscuit industry.

The immigrants from Ruthenia settled in New York, before branching out into neighboring areas. These Muslims organized themselves into the Mohammadan Society of America, with headquarters in Brooklyn, New York. Nyang informs us that an unpublished study done by a Slavic scholar in the U.S. traces their date of entry into the U.S. back to the turn of the century.

Another early group of Muslim immigrants who came and settled were the Muslims from the Punjab in British India. Following in the footsteps of their neighbors, these Muslims responded to the food shortages in Punjab at the turn of the century by coming and settling on the West Coast as farm workers. Willows, California, was one of their early settlements, and today their descendants are scattered in the Western U.S. Some of the Pakistanis and Indian Muslims also settled on the eastern seaboard. Like many other immigrants, they were students, seamen traders, and stowaways who decided to make the U.S. their home away from home. Many of these Muslim immigrants who left their homes of origin did not have much education or means of support back in their own countries and certainly many of them believed that their arrival in the New World would open new avenues of economic opportunities.

Some of these early Muslims were men who seriously believed that they could strike it rich quick in the U.S., and return home, but the slowness, or lack of success in the U.S., or other entanglements soon changed their plans. Others had no intentions of returning home because of the state of affairs they left behind.

In all of these cases, the profound yearning to be successful impelled them into the field of business. Their main areas of business settlements were the states of Michigan, Illinois, New York, Pennsylvania, Iowa, California, and Indiana. The farmlands of the Mid-West and Far-West attracted those who were of rural backgrounds from the Levant, Crescent.

The Arabs and Albanians preferred the Mid-West while the pre-independence Indian Muslims from the Punjab area were inclined towards the California farmlands, where their knowledge of agricultural products such as rice and sugar cane became an arrest.

I implore the reader to bear in mind that no attempt on the part of these early ethnic Muslims was directed toward introducing the downtrodden African-American to Islam. Despite the fact that some of them set up small businesses in the African-American community, when it came to religious education, they completely ignored the African-American. It is also important to note that some of them openly violated the creeds of Islam by selling alcohol, pork, and lucky charms -- all in hopes of achieving the American dream of wealth.

It behooves those African-Americans who are aspiring to culturally identify with the Arabs and other ethnic Muslims to historically examine why there was no effort on the part of the Arabs, Indians, and even Africans to introduce Islam to the African-American community.

Take note that it was not until Noble Drew Ali and Elijah Muhammad (more notably Elijah Muhammad) started their movements that these various ethnic Muslims raised a loud voice about correct (Orthodox) Islam in the African-American community.

Despite some divisions along national lines, attempts were constantly made by other concerned Muslims to gather these isolated Muslims into a compact organizational structure. After Detroit and New York City came Pittsburgh, Cleveland, Worcester, Boston and Providence. Work in Detroit was begun in 1917, and there were four societies in the Detroit-Windsor area. By 1920, centers were operating in Michigan City, Indiana, Chicago, Toledo, Cedar Rapids, Milwaukee, Akron, Philadelphia, and Baltimore.[3]

---

[3] Ibid., pp. 339.

As a result of these previous activities, there were several organizations serving the Muslims in the U.S. Presently, there is the Council of Imams (teachers) in North America, which includes fifteen teacher-scholars in the U.S. The Federation of Islamic Associations, in the U.S. and Canada, holds an annual convention and publishes the Muslim Star. Furthermore, within the five years, a number of other Islamic organizations have emerged.

One of the first known attempts to institute Islam among African-Americans minus black nationalist trappings was initiated by Sheikh Dau'wd. Sheikh Dau'wd established the Islamic Mission of America, in Brookland, New York in 1928 for the defense and propagation of Islam.

He was granted a charter by Shaikd Khalid of Jordan and King Saad of Saudi Arabia, which reaffirmed his right to establish an Islamic mission in the Western Hemisphere. Sheikh Dau'wd taught his congregation that they were the children of Adam, the heirs and descendants of Abraham, Ismail, Isaac, and Jacob. According to some Islamic journals, Dau'wd established the first Islamic school in America. More will be said about him later.

The next attempt, according to research by Dr. Sulayman Nyang, was a Muslim organization called the African Muslim Welfare Society of America (AMWSA). It was founded in 1927. This organization was incorporated in 1928 as a religious body in Pittsburgh, Pennsylvania.

The organization consisted of mostly Arab Muslims, but it also tried to recruit African Americans in the Pittsburgh area. Its leader, a Sudanese by the name of Imam

Muhammad Majid, put forth this noble effort. With the exception of the Ahmadis no other effort, to my knowledge, was made to convert African-Americans to Islam.

Considering the fact that Nobel Drew Ali and Elijah Muhammad introduced Islam to downtrodden African-Americans via black nationalism, it behooves us to investigate in broad scope the history of African Muslims in the Americas as traders, and as slaves. We get the idea of how heavily Africa is populated with Muslims from an article written in the *Islamic Review*, entitled "Africa -- The Muslim Continent." The article states that out of 273 million people, 170 million are Muslims, namely 62 percent of the total population.[4]

With this knowledge one can safely say that prior to slave trading and colonialism, Africa was far more Islamic than the above percentage indicates. A specific date as to when the first African Muslims came to the Americas is not known, but it is well known that Africans in North Africa and South of the Sahara had developed Islamic centers in the Americas prior to the slave trade, and that among the slaves in the United States were a large number of Muslims.

History attests to the fact that Muslim slaves were viewed as superior by slavemasters and other slaves. They

---

[4] In Amullah Khan "Africa -- The Muslim Continent", The Islamic Review, Woking England (July-August, 1966), pp. 5.

often resisted acculturation and assimilation, and they were often educated, and clung to their faith.

Dr. Terry Alford has utilized his sword-like pen and research genius to compel us to accept these hard to believe facts in his illustrious book, *Prince Among Slaves*, which concerns itself with an African Muslim Prince who was forced into slavery by conveying the following information:

> *The fact of his person's royal heritage was, presumably, well known, since records showed that the man was called "Prince" while a slave at Natchez. But his true name was Abraham, or as it would be pronounced among his own people, who were African Muslims, Ibrahima. He claimed to have been born in Timbuktu, the son of a powerful monarch, and educated there and elsewhere in Africa in the way common at the time to Islamic communities throughout the world. I learned that in 1788, when he was twenty-six and a colonel in his father's army, Ibrahima had been defeated in a war, captured, and sold to a slave-ship captain who brought him to the West Indies. During the summer of that year he was purchased by a Natchez farmer named Thomas Foster, and for the next four decades he was Foster's slave on a plantation near the city. Despite his extreme misfortune, Ibrahima adhered to a strict, self-imposed code of conduct throughout that time, never drinking, stealing, or being found guilty of a breach of confidence or trust.*

Alford continues by telling us that there were two men who met the Prince later in life and gave strong testimony to his intellectual prowess.   One, whose name is not known, thought him "well versed in Oriental literature", perspicacious, and eloquent. The second, John Frederick Schroeder, an American knowledgeable in Eastern languages, wrote, "He is very familiar with the Koran, many passages of which he read for me with correctness and fluency." Ibrahima, Schroeder remarked, "read and wrote Arabic for me by the hour."[5]

The following is the text of a passport that was given to Ibrahima by Henry Clay, the Secretary of State. An interesting point is, a number of respectable people were earnestly seeking Ibrahima's release from bondage. The substance of this passport unequivocally proves that.[6]

*Department of State*
*Washington, 17th January 1829*

*The President of the United States, having been informed that the bearer hereof, Abduhl Rahhahman, was held in a state of slavery by a citizen of the United States, that he was of Moorish descent, and a person of much consideration in his native country of Africa, and that his emancipation from slavery would be very agreeable to the Emperor of Morocco, the undersigned Secretary of State of the United States was directed by the President to adopt measures for liberation of the before-mentioned Moor, Abduhl Rahhahman, and for his transportation to his family and connections and native*

---

[5] Terry Alford, <u>Prince Among Slaves</u> (New York: Harcourt Brace Jovanovich, 1977), pp. xvi & 13-14.

[6] <u>Ibid.</u>, pp. 56.

*country.  His manumission was accordingly procured
from the citizen of the United States who held him as a
slave, and he came to this City, at the public's expense,
last spring.  It was the President's intentions to have
him transported to Tangier, to be delivered to the
Emperor of Morocco, but as Abduhl Rahhahman prefers
going to the American Colony of Liberia, on the coast
of Africa, from whence he expects to be able to reach
his relations, the President yields to his desire, and
accordingly he proceeds to Norfolk, in company of his
wife, to obtain, at the expense of the United States, a
passage in the ship Harriet, a vessel chartered by the
American Colonization Society, which is preparing to
sail for Liberia, about the 20th of this month.*

*In testimony of the foregoing I have hereunto set
my hand and affixed the Seal of the Department of
State this 17th day of January, in the year of our
Lord 1829.*

*H. Clay*

---

Alford by way of careful historical investigation points
out that the positive attitude among large members of slave
owners toward selected Muslim slaves, such as Ibrahima,
was eventually displayed to other Muslim slaves as well.

*Each slaveholder was pretty well free to do what
he wished about Islamic practice on his plantation.
It could be an important decision.  The annual fast
(Ramadan), the dietary rules (no pork), and the work
lost due to the frequent prayers of a practicing
Muslim required forbearance from an owner.  Ayuba*

*Sulayman, was a Pullo who was a slave on Kent Island in the Chesapeake Bay in 1730, was mocked and had dirt thrown in his face when he prayed. Just as common, however, were examples of indulgence. The Muslims were to Western eyes, certainly, the most intelligent of the Africans brought to North America. "The active and intellectual principles of the Africans have never been completely unfolded, except perhaps in the case of the Foolahs . . ., a great part of the Mandingoes, and one or two other tribes", wrote Carl Wadstrom, who visited Gambia in 1788. True or not, the planters agreed, for they turned to the Muslims for drivers, overseers, and confidential servants with a frequently their numbers did not justify. It is not surprising that George Proffitt, a major New Orleans slave trader who had a wide variety of Africans from which to pick, had "Big Jack, a Mandingo, 30 years old", as his overseer and thought him a very good one. Sober, self-disciplined, and generally honest, a Muslim could be so useful that a planter might give him berth solely for financial advantage.*[2]

As was stated earlier, the Muslim slave felt superior to other slaves, as well as to the slave owners. This attitude can be attributed to the reasons why they accepted overseer positions. As we know, the Quran prohibits this kind of superior attitude, but the reader, or student of history must remember that tribalism is somewhat endemic to the African experience. Therefore, the temperament of religious superiority coupled with tribal arrogance is what

---

[7] Ibid., pp. 174 & 175.

enabled the Muslim slave to accept these condescending positions.

Ayuba Sulayman was commonly referred to as Job, as will be discussed later in this chapter.

Dr. Alford has undoubtedly given history and the African-American some invaluable information.     His academic objectivity is highly commendable.  The history of the Muslim slave is treated with concern, care, and intellectual perseverance.  At long last the African Muslim is placed in proper perspective.

I should also mention that other scholars have shown us that people of Mali sent trading expeditions to America and made cultural contributions to the new world in pre-Columbian times.  Whether free or enslaved, the Muslim African made a profound mark on American history.

On this same note, it is my contention that had it not been for Kunte Kinte's Islamic zeal and question for freedom, Alex Haley would not have been nationally and internationally known.  Kunte Kinte, by way of his Islamic belief, maintained a proud family legacy.  It was common practice for the slave owners, in their hatred of Islam, to try to break the will and spirit of the Muslim slaves.

As a result, decrees were eventually passed by the United States government that no more Muslims could be brought to America enslaved because of their obstinate determination for freedom; also, because of the influence they had on other slaves.  Slaves on the plantation could not practice the Islamic religion, nor could they retain their names or pass their Islamic names on to their children, nor could they pray or teach their language or religion to their children.

If they were caught doing any of these things they could be put to death or severely punished. The plan to stop Islam from reaching the American continent is recorded in the first document concerning the importation of black slaves into the Western Hemisphere issued by King Fernando the Catholic on September 16, 1501. He gave general instructions to Sir Nicolas Ovando, the newly appointed Governor of the Indies, enjoining him "not to allow to enter into the colonies any Muslims; but to permit to come black slaves, with the condition that they be born under Christian power."

These royal decrees stressed that black slaves brought to the American continent had to be natives of parts of Guinea, for African Muslims (Moors) had been involved in Spain in actual rebellions against their enslavement, incidents that were assigned, primarily to the profundity of Islamic influence. The ones from Guinea, on the contrary, were considered totally deprived of religion, if they professed something that resembled religion, it was only ridiculous superstitions that they did not practice when they came to the Americas, especially the United States.

Dr. Leslie B. Rout Jr. has utilized Spanish terminology to describe certain slaves who were accepted or prohibited from entering the Western Hemisphere, based on the declaration of these royal decrees.

*A 1522 rebellion of bondsmen in Santo Domingo touched off a review of royal policy, and the conclusion was that combination of Muslim-*

*influenced gelfes and disgruntled ladinos had been responsible for this frightening challenge to white authority. The further shipment of either ladinos or gelofes to America was therefore declared an illegal action. The prohibition was followed by decrees on 25 February 1530 and 13 September 1532 that specifically proscribed the dispatch of any white, moorish, jewish, or ladino slave to the indies. Only African bozales who were not gelofes were to be disembarked because they were considered "peaceful and obedient."*[8]

Also, according to Rout, Africans from upper Guinea were often subcategorized as gelofes, biafras, and mandigos.

**Ladino:**   A Christianized African slave who spoke Spanish or had some knowledge of Spanish culture.

**Bozal:**   A slave brought directly to the new world from Africa or therefore, neither Christianized nor Spanish-speaking.

**Gellofes:**   A mass of sub-saharan slaves in Spain after 1462 by the Portuguese were designated Negroes de jalof (gelofes), meaning that their alleged places of embarkation were

---

[8] Leslie B. Rout Jr., The African Experience in Spanish America, (New York: Cambridge University Press, 1976), pp. 24-26, 16, xiv, xv.

stations somewhere between the Senegal river and Sierra Leone.

To add to the above, some historians have stated that the civil war that was raging in Nigeria in 1802 contributed heavily to a Muslim population in America. Slave ships had been coming to the Nigerian coast since the 17th Century. The civil war was between Muslim of the North and Christians of the South. It was supposedly started because some of the Muslims had been captured by the Nigerian Christians and sold to white slave traders. Slave traders were instrumental in systematically instigating the war for the purpose of acquiring slaves for the New World.

Many of these slaves who escaped were Muslims, who in turn found refuge with the Indians, namely, the Seminoles. Some established residential centers in the South, Savannah, Georgia being one that accepted large numbers of these escaped Muslim slaves. Also, the sea-coast island people had a large number of Muslims in their population.

The fact that these escaped Muslim slaves settled on sea-coastal areas is or can be attributed largely to their maritime traditions. It is speculated that these Muslim slaves interacted with the Seminoles to the extent that a cross-cultural exchange took place. Edwin C. Reynolds describes it in this manner:

> *The Negro slave dresses very much like the Seminoles, scantily when they were at work in their fields but with colorful splendor of adornment -- turbans and shawls, smocks, moccasins and leggings, glittering metal ornaments -- when they were bent*

*upon the enjoyment of a festive occasion. The Seminole Negroes were interpreters, farmers -- in fact, they had more knowledge of soil cultivation than the Seminoles. Also, they established a separate town in the West.*[9]

*According to some Muslim scholars and the dictionary, a turban is primarily a Muslim headdress.*

According to J. A. Rogers, Osceola (Seminole chief) married an African woman, it was her capture as a slave in 1836, which led to the second Seminole War.[10]  In 1836, President Jackson told General Sidney Jessup to get all the Seminoles on reservations and all blacks back on the slave plantations.   Thousands of slaves had escaped to the Seminole nation.  Thousands more had been taken from plantations in raids by the Seminoles and their Muslim allies.  President Jackson told  General Jessup that if the Seminoles refused to give up the slaves and return to the reservations, he should exterminate them all.

In 1835, the Seminoles had plenty of land, plenty of cattle and a standing army of well-trained ex-slaves who had been war prisoners (experiencing soldiers).   The Seminoles fought a seven year long war in Florida against the entire United States Army.  The Seminoles were also

---

[9] Edwin C. Reynolds The Seminoles (University of Oklahoma Press, 1957), pp. 48.

[10] J. A. Rogers 100 Amazing Facts about The Negro (Helga M. Rogers, New York, N.Y., 1957), pp. 16.

successful in freeing thousands of slaves and getting many of them out of the country into neighboring islands, where many of their descendants still live. Suffice it to say, that in addition to the Seminoles, the slaves in general, and the Muslims slaves in particular left an indelible mark on the war with the U.S. Army. The following statement should sum it up better than I can say it:

*We have at no former period in our history, had to contend with so formidable enemy. No Seminole proves false to his country (Florida) nor has a single instance occurred of a first rate warrior having surrendered.*

-- General Thomas Sidney Jessup. United States Army Commander in Florida in 1837.

Again, I am attributing a certain amount of the Seminoles' valor to the escaped Muslim slaves, who had a natural propensity to fight for freedom. I know this is an untenable position to some, but my acquaintance with the Muslims in history compels me to accept such a position.

Moreover, Professor Basil Davidson further suggests that many of the maritime merchants were learned men of Islam who followed a tradition of voyaging up and down the New World. These African Muslim traders established harmonious relations with the indigenous population (Indians), which subsequently influenced their familial acceptance of the African traders when they voluntarily and involuntarily took up residence in the New World.

Davidson also writes that these sea-faring people were from the Mali and Songhay Empires and they subsequently succeeded in establishing colonies throughout the Americas. He continues to enhance our knowledge on this subject by conveying the following important and significant information.

> *An African scholar, Al Omari, in a work published in Cairo about 1342, tells of mariners of the Mali Empire crossing the Atlantic Ocean to the New World during the reign of Mansa Musa I. We are informed that "Omari in the tenth chapter of his "Masalik al Absar, reproduces a story which suggests that Atlantic voyages were made by mariners of West Africa in the times of the Emperor Kankan Musa of Mali; and which roundly states that the predecessor of Kankan Musa embarked on the Atlantic with two thousand ships, and sailed westward and disappeared.*[11]

We can safely say, based on historical evidence, that Muslim contact with America dates back a few hundred years.

Additionally, Professor Leo Wiener also made use of historical, linguistic, and cultural evidences to convince us of the influences of the Africans in Ancient America before Columbus. Professor Leo Wiener was a Harvard scholar who published a three-volume work about the Arabic-Mandingo influence in the New World which caused an unrestrained furor among academicians in the 1920's.

---

[11] Basil Davidson, <u>Lost Cities of Africa</u>, (Little, Brown & Company, 1959), pp. 74.

He was a philologist who made use of available lexicology to trace important contributions to America back to Arab-African roots. He mistakenly believed that it was solely the Arab cultural milieu which was vicariously carried by Africans, who in turn, potentiated American civilization.

He failed to see that the African and his strong belief in Islam was the contributing force that touched every people or culture that they came in contact with. Nevertheless, his work is highly valuable. We must cite some of the findings from the conclusion of Wiener's massive work/

*The presence of Negroes with their trading masters in America before Columbus is proved by the representation of Negroes in America sculpture and design, by the occurrence of a black nation at Darien early in the XVI century, but more specifically by Columbus' emphatic reference to Negro traders from Guinea, who trafficked in a gold alloy, guanine, of precisely the same composition and bearing the same name, frequently referred to by early writers in Africa. (Arab is interchangeable with Islam).*

*There were several foci from which the Negro traders spread in the two Americas. The eastern part of South America, where the Caribs are mentioned, seems to have been reached by them from the West Indies. Another stream, possibly from the same focus, radiated to North along roads marked by the presence of mounds, and reached as far as Canada. The chief cultural influence was exerted by a Negro colony in Mexico, most likely from Teotihuacan and Tuxtla, who may have been instrumental in establishing the city of Mexico. From here their influence pervaded the neighboring tribes, and ultimately, directly or indirectly, reached Peru. That the Negro civilization was carried chiefly by the trader is proved not only by Columbus specific reference, but also by the presence of the African merchant, the tangoman, as tiangizman in Mexico, hence Aztec tiangiz "market", and by the university of the blue and white shell-money from Canada to LaPlata, and the use of shells in the Peru-Guatemala trade.*

*...The African penetration in religion and civic life and customs was thorough and to judge the survival of the Arabic words in a Malinke or Soninke form in America, especially among the Caraibs and Aztecs, proceeded almost exclusively from the Mandingoes, either the ancestors of the present Malinkes, or a tribe in which the Sonike language had not yet completely separated from its Malinke affinities.*[12]

Professor Weiner states further that the American language has its roots in or was largely influenced by the Arabic and Mande:

*Just as in mande, so throughout America, the Arabic habal, in forms derived from Mande boli, represents the idea of spirit or anything related to*

---

[12] Leo Wiener, Vol. III, Africa and the Discovery of America, (Innes and Sons, Philadelphia, PA 19922), pp. 365 & 366.

*religion or medicine, in America, too, the bolitgi, the
masters of the boli, appears as boratio and a large
number of forms linguistically derived from this, with
the identical powers as in Africa and wielding the
gourd rattle, the mitraqah, in Tupi and other South
American languages denominated Maraca.*

*The Mande tigi in the sense of "Master" is also
separately represented in many American languages
and in the appellation cacique, formed by the early
voyages.*

*A thorough investigation of the archeological
remains in the Western Sudan, coupled with a further
painstaking philogical study of the Arab influences in
Africa, may reveal other African elements that are
the prototypes of similar conditions in the civilization
of America.*[13]

Dr. Weiner traces most of the African language roots
back to Arabic. He also states that a form of Islamic
worship was practiced in Mexico:

*It can now be shown that here we have, indeed,
the aman "the faith", for the singing of the prayer at
day-break, to keep off the suba, is course, the Arabic
prayer at day-break.*[14]

---

[13] Wiener, Vol. III, pp. 368-370.

[14] Wiener, Vol. III, pp. 251 & 252.

Considering the above information, we must accept the paradoxical premise that Professors Leo Wiener, Joseph McCabe, James Henry Brested, and Leo Frobenius were caucasian scholars who, for the most part, paved the way for African and African-American historians. These men stood on a foundation of historical truth and declared to the world of academia that Africa and Islam were not barbaric and barren. We should constantly thank these men of integrity and intellectual insight.

Before I journey into black nationalist territory, I must cite some more historical information pertaining to the Islamic belief of the slaves. Afterwards, I will discuss two early black nationalist figures. Both of these individuals have Islamic interests and an Islamic family lineage. However, the importance of my present historical itinerary demands that I continue to cite those highly cultivated African Muslim slaves. Professor Morroe Berger gave us greater knowledge about our subject; in fact, he heightens the issue to irrefutable acceptance. In his attempt to understand the existence of the Nation of Islam, Professor Berger notes that Muslim slaves tended to be viewed as superior by both themselves and other slaves; they were often educated, and they resisted acculturation and assimilation, thus retaining their faith longer. Professor Berger also maintains that, while no definite connection can be made between Twentieth Century black Muslims and those who might have survived the slave era, there might be some possible connection: "It is quite possible that some of the various American Muslim groups of the past half century or so had their roots in these vestiges, that the tradition was handed down in a weak chain from generation to generation."[15]

Accounts of a number of these highly cultivated Muslim slaves were collected and preserved by three noted ethnologists of the nineteenth century. Theodore Dwight, William Brown Hodgson, and James Hamilton Couper. The most distinguished was Dwight, a grandson of Jonathan Edwards, nephew of one president of Yale and cousin of another who served as recording secretary of the American Ethnological Society.

Dwight took a strong definitive position on the so-called notion of African inferiority; insisting upon the high level of Muslim civilization in Africa, and telling the stories of a number of Muslim slaves he had met. "Among the victims of the slave trade among us," he wrote, "have been men of pure and exalted characters, who have been treated like beasts of field by those who claimed a purer religion."

William B. Hodgson, also mentions five Muslim slaves in a 1852 work. One, Bul-Ali, was a slave-driver on a Sapelo Island, Georgia, plantation. Also C.C. Jones, a missionary who authored "The Religious Instruction of the Negroes in the United States", noted that Muslim slaves, under pressure from Christianizing forces, would devise accommodations to the new faith by equating God with Allah and Jesus with Muhammad.

---

[15] Morroe Berger, "The Black Muslims", Horizon 6, January, 1964, pp. 49-64.

Undoubtedly the most interesting story that has survived concerns one Job, son of Solomon, who was born around 1701 in the kingdom of Futa near the Gambia river.

*In the possession of Michael Denton of Maryland there was found a slave who observed the custom of praying five times a day according to the requirements of the Mohammedan religion. An ignorant white boy, seeing him kneel and bowing in the direction of Mecca, threw sand in his eyes and so impaired his sight as to invite an investigation of his habits. It was discovered he was an orthodox Mohammedan and an Arabic scholar. Hearing this, James Oglethorpe interceded in his behalf, had him liberated and taken to England. There he was accorded all of the honors due a man of learning. He was associated with a professor of Cambridge in the translation of Oriental manuscripts and through him he was introduced to some of the most desirable people of England. This was probably the record of Job, a slave in Maryland in 1731-1733, a Fula brought from Futa in which is now French Senegal. He could write Arabic and repeat the whole Koran. He also became friendly with Sir Hans Sloane, president of the Royal Society, for whom he translated a number of Arabic inscriptions.*[16]

---

[16] The Negro in Our History, by Carter G. Woodson, The Associated Publishers, Inc., Washington, D.C. (copyright 1947), pp. 33.

(See Thomas Bluett: *Some Memoirs of the Life of Job the Son of Solomon the High Priest of Boonda in Africa*; London 1816)

There is an interesting parallel between Ayuba (Job) Ibn Sulaiman and Ibrahima, both were highly considered for their decorum, integrity, intelligence, and strong independence of mind. Both were given their freedom because of these factors, and more importantly because of their continued devotion to their religion principles.

Concerned persons must consult Mr. Bluett's unique book on Job. He discusses Job's family background, his revered status among Europeans in England, his captivity, and his devotion to his religion. Other scholarly works on the experience and travels of this African Muslim slave are well documented in the following:

Douglass Grant, *The Fortunate Slave*, (London, 1968); Phillip C. Curtin, ed., *Africa Remembered, Narratives by West Africans from the Era of the Slave Trade*, (Madison, 1967), pp. 17-59; Francis Moore, *Travels into Inland Parts of Africa*, (London, 1738). Also, an interesting description of the life of Job is given in Dr. Folarin Shyllon's study on *Black People in Britain, 1955-1833*, (London, New York, and Ibadan; Oxford University Press, 1977).

Interestingly, Dr. Shyllon compares the grave experiences of Job with those of other blacks whose misfortune landed them in Britain.

# Islam in South America and the Caribbean

$\mathbf{M}$any Muslim slaves from the Western Sudan were transported to South America, the Caribbean and Brazil; according to Nina Rodrigues and Gilberto Freyre, these countries received a substantial number. Furthermore, they believe that not only the Bahian movement of 1835, but other slave-hut revolts have been affiliated with the religious organizations of the Muslims from West Africa. They attribute great importance to the influence exercised over the Yorubus (known in Brazil as Nagos) and the Ewes by the Muslim Fulahs and Hausas. These Muslims from the West African kingdoms of Wurno, Sokoto, and Gando were seen by the Portuguese as the aristocrats of the Senzales (slave quarters).

The cultural effect upon the formation of Brazilian society that was exerted by an Islamism brought to Brazil by Muslim slaves was very pronounced and pervasive.

*The Mohammedan Negroes in Brazil, once they have been distributed among the slave huts of the colonial Big House, did not lose contact with Africa, nor did the Negro fetishist fail to keep in touch with the advanced cultural areas of their native continent. The Nagos, for example, from the kingdom of Yoruba, as well as the Mohammedans, went to the trouble of importing religious objects and articles for personal use: kola nuts, cauris, cloth and soap from the coast, and oil of the dende palm. Down to the end of the nineteenth century the reparation of Haussa and Nago freedom from Bahia to Africa took place, and it was such freedom -- repatriates who*

*founded in Arda a city by the name of Porto Seguro.
So intimate did the relations between Bahai and
those cities come to be that heads of commercial
houses in Salvador received honorary distinctions
from the government of Dahomey.*[17]

Islam flourished and branched out in Brazil in the form
of a powerful sect that prospered in the dark of the slave
huts, and with teachers and preachers from Africa to give
instruction in reading the books of the Quran in the Arabic,
and with Mohammedan schools and houses of prayer
functioning there. The atmosphere that preceded the
movement of 1835 in Bahia was one of intense religious
ardor among the slaves. In Mata -- Porcos Lane, on the
Praca slope, at St. Francis-Crops, in the very shadow of
the Catholic churches and monasteries and the niches of the
Virgin Mary and St. Anthony of Lisbon, slaves who were
schooled in the Quran preached the religion of the prophet,
setting it over against the religion of Christ that was
followed by their white masters, up above in the Big
Houses. They propagandized against the Catholic mass
saying that it was the same as worshipping a stick of wood;
and to the Christian rosary with its cross of Our Lord they
imposed their own, which was fifty centimeters long, with
ninety-nine wooden beads and with a ball in place of a
crucifix on the end.[18] An interesting point to make at this
juncture is that anti-Catholic prejudices among Muslims
influenced Negroes and Mestizos bias toward

---

[17] Gilberto Freye, <u>The Masters and The Slave</u> (New
York: Alfred A. Knopf, 1946), pp. 310-313.

[18] <u>Ibid</u>., pp. 318 & 319.

Protestantism. Freyre conveys more relevant information pertaining to the cultural impact of the Muslim slaves on Brazilian dress among the women, and the remembrance of religious practices.

In Bahai, in Rio, in Recife, in Minas, African garb, showing the Mohammedan influences, was for a long time worn by the blacks. Especially by the black women who sold sweets and by the vendors of alva. To this day, in the streets of Bahia, one may meet with these negro women, peddling their wares, with their long shawls made of pano da costga, or "cloth from the coast."[19]

Religious remembrances were manifested by way of long prayers, fasting, no alcohol, sacrifices of sheep, vestments consisting of long white tunics.[20]

It is presumed that the African slave, especially the one of Mohammedan origin, very often experienced a genuine repugnance at the unclean habits of his master.[21]

Freyre tells us many things about Muslim slaves in Brazil, but the most important, I think, is the fact that these slaves didn't lose their cultural or religious identity. Furthermore, this identity remembrance was the most significant factor that contributed to the continuous slave rebellions. The one in Bahai was the most profound.

---

[19] Ibid., pp. 314 & 315.

[20] Ibid., pp. 315 & 316.

[21] Ibid., pp. 317.

Again and again, Muslim insurrections broke out in Brazil: in 1757, 1757, and 1772. Five times, from 1807 to 1835, Muslims in Bahai revolted against what their religion did not accept scripturally, slavery of body and of mind.

*These were not mere slave insurrections. These Muslims resented their status as slaves, but more importantly they had immense pride in their Islamic heritage. They, therefore, believed that they were carrying out a holy war that they and their forbearers had waged in Africa. In their Muslim Mosques and in their secret societies, they plotted against blacks who would not join them as well as the whites for whom they harbored a fierce hatred. In 1807, 1809, 1813, and 1816 there were outbreaks in Bahai. In 1813, for example, the Negroes arose one morning at four o'clock, burned the homes of whites as well as their own slave quarters, and killed thirteen whites. They died rather than surrender. In January, 1835, the officials heard of plans of a great uprising. Every precaution, including a search of the black quarters, was taken in order to prevent the uprising. At one place the searching officials were fired on and were overcome. The uprising continued, with many people killed and wounded. It is important to note that the entire city of Bahai was completely terrified.*

The best testimonial to the bravery and courage of these captured black leaders is the fact that instead of being hanged as common criminals they were shot with full military honors. Despite the fact that slavery lasted in Brazil longer than anywhere else in the New World, the blacks never tired of registering the kind of resentment that the Muslims of Bahai showed in 1835.[22]

Professor Michael Turner of the City University of New York has written, "Os Pretos do Africa: Brazilian Slaves in Dahomey," a paper presented at the Graduate Student Conference on the continent of Africa, that the Muslim slaves that returned to Dahomey following the slave trade in Brazil, built the first mosques in the capital. For additional works on Muslim slaves in Brazil, one should pay attention to the works of Manuel Querino, Roger Bastide, J.C. Fletcher, and D.P. Kidder, and John Chandler; also W. Burgess. In addition to the literature on Muslim slaves in Brazil, there are also some interesting materials on Muslim slaves in the Caribbean. Carl Campbell did some research titled *Jonas Mohammed Bath and the Free Mandingoes of Trinidad: The Question of their Repatriation to Africa, Pan African Journal*, Vol. 17, No. 2 (Summer, 1974), pp. 130-133.

Campbell was able to substantiate with ample evidence from the Trinidadian archives that the Muslim slaves were not only very well organized in communities with Mohammed Bah, or Bath, as their Imam and Qadi, but that they were able to buy the freedom of their Muslim brothers by way of pooling their resources.

It was Jonas Mohammed Bath who formed this Mandingo society in Port of Spain. Since he was a man of high rank before his arrival in the island, it

---

[22] John Hope Franklin, From Slavery To Freedom (New York: Alfred A. Knopf, 1963), pp. 123 & 124.

is possible that he played a prominent part in the life of this group even before his emancipation.

Bath's own description of his magisterial role, corroborated by one of his countrymen, Tode, and also by John Newbold, 2nd Alcalde of the Cabildo of Port of Spain, was this . . . he hears and decides all differences and disputes in relation to debts, property or otherwise, that all the people of that faith and nation obey and observe all the orders, directions and decisions which he makes upon matters in dispute between them, they are brought under his notice, whether in his character or priest or of magistrate.

Campbell maintains that these Muslim slaves were completely engrossed in plans to return to Africa. Furthermore, they were extremely resentful of their enslavement by Christian infidels. They tried to duplicate in Trinidad many of the cultural practices known to them in Africa. Paradoxically, many of these Muslims in the territory of Trinidad prospered and functioned as free men and women in their small and somewhat insecure society. The reader should also study the works of Sulayman S. Nyang, *The Islamic Identity in the United States of America*; also *Islam in the United States of America: A Review of the Sources*.

There have also been some sketchy writings about Muslims in Jamaica; some of these writings are concerned with communication between the Muslims in Jamaica and their homeland. The letter that follows was translated by an Englishman who spent twelve months in the West Indies. R.R. Madden tells us about his encounter with Abubacarr Saddiq and the latter's decision to give him autobiographical fragments written in Arabic.  One of the letters is as follows:

*Abu Bakr al -Siddiq to Muhammad Kaba*
*Kingston, Jamaica, October 18, 1834*

*Dear Countryman,*

*I now answer your last letter, my name, in Arabic, is Abon Becr Sadiki, and in Christian language, Edward Doulan, I born in Timbuktu, and brought up in Jenne; I finished read the Coran in the country of Bouna, which place I was taken captive in war.  My master's name in this country is Alexander Anderson. Now my countryman, God hath given me a faithful man, a just and good master, he made me free; and I know truly that he has shown mercy to every poor soul under him.  I know he has done that justice which our King William the Fourth commanded him to do (God save the King) and may he be a conqueror over all his enemies, from east to west, from north to south, and the blessing of God extend over all his kingdom, and all his ministers and subjects.  I beseech you, Mohomed Caba, and all my friends, continue in praying for my friend, my life, and my breadfruit, which friend is my worthy Dr. Madden, and I hope that God may give him honour, greatness, and gladness, and likewise his generation to come, as long as Heaven and Earth stands.  Now my countryman, these prayers that I request of you is greater to me than any thing else I can wish of you, and also you must pray that God may give him strength and power to overcome all his enemies, and that the King's orders to him be held in his right hand firmly The honour I have in my heart for him is great; but God knows the secrets of all hearts. Dear countryman, I also beseech you to remember in your prayers my master Alexander Anderson, who gave me my liberty free and willingly; and may the Almighty prosper him, and protect him from all dangers.*

*Whenever you wish to send me a letter, write it in Arabic language; then I will understand it properly.*

*I am dear Sir,*
*Your Obedient Servant,*
*Edward Doulan*

---

The translations that were given to Dr. Madden by Abubacarr Saddiq, are now available in reprinted or paraphrased form in Wilson Armistead's *A Tribute to the Negro*, (London, 1848), pp. 245-47; and in The Friends of Africa, 1 (10): 151-153).

In Phillip D. Curtin's *Africa Remembered*, 1967, we get a chance to read the two letters exchanged between Muhammad Kaba and Abubacarr Saddiq, one of which is displayed above. From Madden's *Twelve Months Residence in the West Indies* (2 Vols. London, 1837), 2:199-201.

As stated in the beginning, the resources on African Muslim slaves are very sketchy and limited; however, a concerned scholar should be able to organize a worthwhile project utilizing the material that has been cited. I am sure more information about the impact of Islam on various people in past and contemporary history will be written.

Also, the scope and range of Islam on international political events must be placed in proper context.

Slavery and Christianity are usually harmonious partners in the Western world, particularly in America. However, Islam with its creed of manumission which is rooted in human compassion and human exultation, paved the way for the emancipation of slaves. This factor is what makes Islam a vital religious force.

Slavery of the Muslims, however, was not altogether a hopeless condition. If the slave professed faith in Islam he might become a communicant in that connection, enjoying equality with the richest and the best, accepted on the principles of the brotherhood of man.

This Quranic creed of the brotherhood of man -- even unto the slaves -- produced a relentless fervor in the American Muslim slaves for freedom and justice. The American Muslim slave did not and could not submit to the systematic dehumanization that accompanied slavery. Therefore, his presence in America provoked anger, suspicion, and apprehension on the part of the slavemaster.

Is there any wonder that there were subsequent laws established prohibiting the disembarkation of Muslim slaves on the shores of the Western hemisphere.

The proverbial statement "history is best qualified to reward our research" is situated on a firm foundation of truth; primarily because research compels one to accept the facts as they present themselves. The study of history will also compel one to accept the fact that Muslims contributed to the progressive development of geography. The Muslims were instrumental as well as facilitators in the development of political geography, mathematical geography, and cartography. Geography was paramount to the Muslims because they felt and knew the need for accurate determination of the position of places. The expansion of political power and the establishment of a great brotherhood made knowledge about the lands of Islam one of ever-increasing concern.

When the Muslims came into contact with Africa, they met people who were already maritime traders by either tradition, economic necessity, or cultural standards. The Muslims proceeded to develop this practice to the extent that large numbers of African Muslims became even more proficient in the science of travel, trade, and conquest.

Dr. Ivan Van Sertima places my point in proper historical perspective with the following observations:

*The major inventions in maritime navigation that were to transform European shipping during the Renaissance has been made before Christ and were completely lost to Europe during the dark ages. The system of latitudinal and longitudinal coordinates, used as early as 100 B.C. in China, had not, even as late as the Conquest period, been acquired by Europe, whose navigators could not read longitude until the nineteenth century. The lateen sail hoisted on the Spanish and Portuguese caravels came from the Arabs. The astrolabe (an instrument to determine latitude by the sun's altitude), although originally invented by the ancient Greeks, diffused to 15th-Century Europe after passing through centuries of development by the Arabs.*

*Other popular notions that must be dismissed are that Africa had no knowledge of the sea, never had mariners, never made boats, nurtured a landlocked race; that her empires ended at the edge of the desert, unwashed by the world's seas. On the contrary, Africans were navigating the Atlantic before Columbus and Christ. They had moved up the North Atlantic to Ireland, capturing part of that country in a very early period.*[23]

Van Sertima continues by shedding light on the Muslim traders in Asia.

*On the East African coast, along the shores of the Indian Ocean, lies the Bantu-Islamic civilization of the Swahili. These Africans were trading with India and China many centuries before Columbus. In the 13th Century it is recorded that Swahili transhipped an elephant to the court of the Emperor of China as a gift.*[24]

To an extent a large number of these African Muslims became so-called pirates; also, they became great conquerors and culture bearers. They also engaged in

---

[23] Ivan Van Sertima, <u>They Came Before Columbus</u> (Random House, New York, 1976), pp. 55 & 56.

[24] <u>Ibid</u>., pp. 61.

more extensive trade through various parts of Africa and the new world. The following accounts by Professors Ivan Van Sertima, Harold G. Lawrence, and E. W. Bovill attest to the vast trading practices of the Africans in the Americas after the advent of Islam into the African interior.

> *Arab-Islamic influence on medieval Mali, therefore, was very peripheral, but its impact on trade and on traders cannot be denied.  Nearly all traveling traders in West Africa became Muslims.  It was the pragmatic thing to do, since nearly all foreign trade was with the Arabs.  Hence, this explains the many Arabic words that are found in Mandingo trading items.*
>
> *Another Arabic influence may be found in the coats of arms of medieval Sudan.  Most notable of these is the crescent on some Sudanese medieval armor.  It is generally represented by one upward sign, but frequently it has three stars connected with it, or the crescent is repeated two or three times.  This is a characteristic Muslim emblem.  It is also found in medieval Mexico.  The crescent accompanied at the bottom by three stars or crescents is found on many Mexican shields.*[25]

Harold G. Lawrence enhances this subject to a substantial degree with regard to this assertion that African explorers and traders came to the new world long before

---

[25] Ibid., pp. 101.

Columbus and that these seafaring people were natural voyagers.

This maritime tradition explains very well why a number of escaped Muslim slaves settled on coastal areas, found and maintained refugee among the Seminoles in the everglades, and for the most part made Savannah, Georgia their residence.   Interestingly, the seacoast island people, erroneously called Geechee, counted many Muslims among their population.

> *That Africans voyaged across the Atlantic before the era of Christopher Columbus is no recent belief. Scholars have long speculated that a great seafaring nation which sent its ships to the Americas once existed on Africa's west coast...   We can now positively state that the Mandingoes of the Mali and Songhay Empires, and possibly other Africans crossed the Atlantic to carry on trade with the Western Hemisphere Indians, and further succeeded in establishing colonies throughout the Americas.*[26]

In 1050, the King of the Mandingoes was converted to Islam by the Almoravides.

Professor Lawrence states that: "Mali started on the road to world importance during the reign of Sakura (1285-

---

[26] Harold G. Lawrence, <u>African Explorers of the New World</u>, The Crisis Magazine, June-July, 1962. Republished as a monograph by Haryou -- Act. Inc., New York, 1962.

1300), who vastly extended his domain to include much of Mauritania and established diplomatic relations with Morocco."

As a result of this new contact the Malians learned advanced sea-faring techniques and the concept of the earth's rotundity from such Muslim geographers and astronomers as Abu Zaid, Masudi, Idrisi, Istakhri, Abulfeda, and others.

Lawrence also mentions that both Idrisi and Abulfeda stressed the rotundity of the earth and Abulfeda spoke of voyages around the world.

Thus, it could very well have been that the people of Mali opened the way for West African trade relations with the American Indians when Columbus was not yet born.

In the 15th Century the Songhay Empire under the leadership of Askia Muhammad Toure resumed or continued trade relations with the American Indians. Proof of this, say Lawrence, "is evidenced by the fact that Columbus was informed by some men, when he stopped at one of the Cape Verde Islands off the coast of Africa, that black Muslims had been known to set out into the Atlantic from the Guinea coast in canoes loaded with merchandise steering towards the west."

Reiterating the point, the knowledge of geography and the methodological use of this knowledge enabled the Muslim traders, and merchants to make their presence known and felt throughout the new world. Furthermore, Muslim traders, merchants, and escaped slaves were always interested in establishing their own communities, their own system of trading, and their own commercial exchange organization.   E.W. Bovill gave two very interesting and contrasting stories of a Muslim trader and some Muslim seafaring adventurers (pirates).

*In 1874, the first Moroccan merchant was reported to have arrived at St. Louis to explore the possibilities of developing a trade between his town and the French posts of the Niger, and by the 1880's most of the developing ports of West Africa were connected with Europe by steamship lines.   The trans-Saharan route between Timbuktu and Morocco was certainly much shorter in simple mileage than the route from Timbuktu to St. Louis and from St. Louis by sea to the ports of Morocco, but the new route was infinitely safer, and eventually probably cheaper and swifter.   Still more important was the fact that the new links with the sea put the countries of the Western Sudan in touch with markets they had never known before: From these markets in Europe and America came a demand for agricultural products of the Sudan, and especially for groundnuts (peanuts).*[27]

*In the 17th Century the replacement of the galley by the square-rigged sailing ship opened to the Corsairs a much wider field for their raids.   They were assisted in their more distant enterprises by the numbers of English seamen who, thrown out of*

---

[27] E. W. Bovill, The Golden Trade of the Moors, New York, Oxford University, 1968; also titled, Caravans of the Old Sahara, pp. 249.

*employment when the turbulent days of Elizabeth gave place to the peaceful reign of James I, sought to serve with the Corsairs to save themselves from hunger. Equipped with better ships and experienced navigators, the African pirates began raiding the shores of Britain, Denmark, and Ireland. In the reign of Charles II the Sabee rovers seized and occupied Lundy Island, and the people of Cork shuddered as the call of the Muezzin echoed over the peaceful waters of their harbour.*[28]

For more information on the Muslim (Moors) presence in ancient Britain, I encourage the reader to investigate the re-published work of David MacRitchie entitled *Ancient and Modern Britons, Volumes I and II* .

Christopher Columbus was also informed by the indians of Hispaniola when he arrived in the West Indies that they had been able to obtain gold from Africans who had come from across the sea from the south and southeast. The dates of these accounts coincide precisely with the time that Askia the Great held sway over Songhay., It must also be added that Amerigo Vespucci on his voyage to the Americas witnessed these same Africans Muslims out in the Atlantic returning to Africa.

Interestingly, when the Spanish conquistadors arrived, they found tribes of Africans and African Muslims dispersed all over the New World. The largest African colony was a permanent settlement at Darien where Balboa who saw them in 1513 reported them at war with

---

[28] Ibid., pp. 250.

neighboring Indians. This report was made before the first importation of African slaves to the Antilles, and before any colonies were founded.

Professor Lawrence also points out that there were other African colonies in Northern Brazil among the Charuas.

The reason for citing these different sources which essentially reiterates the facts and points continuously, and to a certain degree needlessly, was based on the fact that the history of Islamic influences on early America is one of the most neglected areas of history. Very few people know of the Islamic traditions and influences brought to these shores from Morocco, Senegal, Gambia, and other Islamic lands. As was stated before, these Muslims -- merchants, traders and slaves were from maritime families.

They were also from a society with advanced political and literary cultures, and because of this and other elated reasons, they regarded their enslavement by the Spanish, the Americans, and the Portuguese, who, according to them, were of lesser sophistication, as not only unacceptable, but demeaning. This feeling of self-dependence and self-importance can undoubtedly be attributed to the African's Islamic upbringing. Their religious background is what engendered their bitterness and hatred of the slave system and their relentless determination to either escape or bring it down.

The reader is encouraged to read a more expansive work on Muslims in America by Dr. Allen Austin entitled *African Muslims in Antebellum America: A Sourcebook.* Austin discusses Islam in Africa, Islam in the New World, and narratives from 50 slaves, 16 of whom are presented in detail, and documents pertaining to relatives of Kunte Kinte. Austin also discusses in some detail some of the same Muslim personalities that this writer discusses.

His historical treatment of Job Ben Solomon, Salili Bilali, and Abdul Rahahman are very impressive. He also discusses two teachers in Africa -- Lamen Kebe and Umar Said, who left large numbers of documents in Arabic. One was a slave in Brazil, the other was enslaved by the Arabs, the Russians, and the Turks.

One lived in Georgetown in Washington, D.C. and the other became a slave in South Carolina. Both, according to Dr. Austin, continued to be practicing Muslims.

The preface of another chapter shares with the reader the lives of six Muslims in Jamaica -- all literate in Arabic. Dr. Austin's book is not only highly informative, but is long overdue.

Slavery in the Iberian peninsula present the black slaves as being common, and the laws affecting them were well developed. Therefore, in the colonies of Spain and Portugal, while the slave was the lowest person in the social order, he was still a human being, with some rights, and some means by which he might achieve freedom. Only the United States made a radical split with the tradition in which all men, even slaves, had certain inalienable rights.

It is extremely important to indicate that slavery took its most peculiar and brutal form in the United States. It took this form primarily because there were no laws or precedent either in tradition or in common law that could paralyze such an inhuman practice. Catholic Portugal and Spain had seen slavery as a natural condition of man; in these feudal societies, freedom was conditional for every man. Furthermore, there was a whole series of gradations of status from slavery to freedom.

Protestant England and America, however, saw slavery as completely unnatural; an important point to remember is that serfdom had been abolished some time before, and slavery had been unknown since Roman times. Therefore, introducing slavery into a society of so-called free men thus posed a real dilemma; how justify slavery in a society based, as the philosopher John Locke had argued, on a contract among free men?

The dilemma was resolved very neatly through an appeal to the Africans alleged inferiority. If the blacks were inherently inferior, if they lacked the capacity to be free men, then slavery could be justified and indeed defended as a service to the slaves themselves, as well as to the masters. And the rules and practices that developed out of this rationale in turn created a system that made the slaves into dependent, servile, infantile creatures, who indeed seemed incapable of exercising freedom.

Slavery enabled the English and the Americans to successfully engage in the exploitation of the New World; therefore, slaves were no longer merely taken over as a sequel of, but also became an object of commerce to supply the colonies with cheap labor. The concept of the Christian world stood on the foundation that, although it was contrary to an unwritten law to enslave a Christian, this principle was not applicable to the unconverted blacks. Forced later from this position when numerous blacks accepted Christianity, they salved their consciences by a peculiar philosophy of the officials of the church. These ecclesiastics held that conversion did not work manumission in the case of the blacks who differed so widely from the white race.

It was precisely this religio-social concept that brandished the African-American as a non-entity -- a concept that religiously justified his enslavement, and socially relegated him to a position of a beast that should be scorned and shunned. It was this religious and social concept that gave birth to an opposing and alternative religious-political concept that vicariously gave the African-American a sense of superiority to caucasian Americans.

In the following chapter I shall look at both of these concepts and determine how they shaped and molded the character, personality, and mind of its adherents. Islam was the religious concept that counter-acted the white man's version of Christianity and its white image of God (Jesus), nationalism was a political and economic concept that restored the African-Americans social framework vis-a-vis an African identity based on African soil. There were also attempts to transform Christianity so that it would harmoniously coincide with the political doctrine of black nationalism.

As promised earlier, I shall now discuss two early black nationalist personalities whose family backgrounds were Islamic, and whose practices were clearly those of a nationalist mode.

# Islam and Black Nationalism

The noted shipbuilder, captain, philanthropist, and nationalist Paul Cuffee, descended from the Muslim community of Ghana. His father was brought to these shores at 11 years of age, his father's name was Saiz Kufu, Kofi, and Koffee are common surnames in Ghana. His father's name was anglicized under the tutelage of Solocum to Cuffee. Immediately after reaching adulthood, and acquiring wealth, Cuffee became engrossed in Africa and African repatriation. He dedicated his life and fortune to this venture.

He circumnavigated Africa eighteen times, crossed it from east to west three times, and from north to south once. Paul Cuffee was the first black to petition the powers that be in regard to slavery. His document was addressed to the legislatures of New Jersey asking that body to petition the Congress of the United States that every slave be freed and that every colored man that so desired be allowed to leave America. This petition led to the American Colonization Society.

Interestingly, this was the first manifestation of black nationalism in America -- it had its greatest impact on Marcus Mosiah Garvey in the 1920's. For more on Paul Cuffee the reader should consult Sheldon H. Harris, *Paul Cuffee: Black American and the African Return*, (Simon & Schuster, New York, 1972).

The American Colonization Society was founded in 1817, just before Paul Cuffee died. With funds from white philanthropists and support from the federal and some of the state governments, it founded Liberia, adjacent to Sierra Leone, in West Africa. The society's primary objective was to put free blacks where they could best use their civilized talents for the benefit of themselves and Africa. Before the civil war, the society transported 13,000 African-Americans to Liberia, most of whom were ex-slaves whose masters freed them for the purpose of emigration.

For more on the American Colonization Society, and early black nationalist movements, see Edwin Redkey, *Black Exodus: Black Nationalism and Back to Africa Movements, 1890-1910.*

Another nationalist who was directly related to Paul Cuffee, and who was also an able captain ,was one Harry Dean. Captain Dean founded the first black nautical training school in America. Captain Dean's family came from Quata, Morocco, for three generations they had been wealthy merchants in Philadelphia. Harry Dean maintained the family Muslim tradition first during his seafaring days aboard the Pedro Gorino and later in Southern Africa where he sought to build an African empire.

He appealed to such leading Pan-Africanists as W.E.B. DuBois, but they refused to support such a concrete effort of Pan-Africanism on native soil. A point of information that should be made is that Dean was not only associated with the Muslim Mosque of London, England, but later distributed Islamic literature in Chicago, Los Angeles, Seattle, and Washington.

The following are two very significant quotes from Dean:

*I am an African and proud of it. There's not a drop of white blood in my veins. My ancestors have been sea captains and merchants and I have spent my life at sea.*

Captain Dean felt that the word Negro is of false derivation, indescriptive, and in every way unfit for the position it fills in our language. He claims that "there is no Negro race, only many African races."

From the union of Susan Cuffee and John Dean, Harry Dean was born, November 20, 1864.

For more on Captain Harry Dean the reader should consult, *The Pedro Gorino*, by Captain Harry Dean & Sterling North (Houghton Mifflin Company, 1929).

Black nationalism was not only subordinate to Islam, but to Christianity as well. It's interesting to note that nationalism found its highest expression by way of Islam. A number of Christian nationalist or Pan-Africanists embraced the basic creed of black nationalism -- the concept that black people should repudiate the white man and his culture; the emotional acceptance and propagation of black culture or race pride. Black nationalists reconstruct history to demonstrate that black men are descended from noble and glorious ancestors, from wise and powerful rulers and conquerors. Black Nationalism also exhorts the black man -- whether free or enslaved -- to stand in defense of his manhood and to manifest exceptional manly strength on behalf of his woman's honor.

Some early Christian nationalists picked up the torch of freedom and rebellion after the Muslim slave's legacy had subsided and subsequently disappeared. Reverend Henry Highland Garnett called upon the slaves to stand up and be men. He encouraged the nearly four million slaves to refuse to work if not granted their freedom. But if they failed, if the masters visited death upon those engaged in work stoppages then:

*You had better all die -- die immediately, than live slaves and entail your wretchedness upon your posterity. However much you and all of us desire it, there is not much hope of redemption without the shedding of blood.... No oppressed people have ever secured their liberty without resistance. What kind of resistance you had better make, you must decide by the circumstances that surround you....*

David Walker, with a voice imprisoned in the determination for black emancipation gave his appeal to arms for slave insurrection. Walker's *Appeal* was reflective of his innate inclination for the love and appreciation of freedom. Many of these nationalists, some might call them revolutionaries, sustained and invoked a principle of insurrection against slavery that was ingrained in the African personality.

In searing words, Walker made slaveholders, racists and hypocrites tremble before the promise of black terror:

*... and believe this, that it is no more harm for you to kill a man who is trying to kill you than it is for you to take a drink of water when thirsty; in fact, the man who will stand still and let another man murder*

*him, is worse than an infidel, and, if he has common
sense, ought not to be pitied....*

David Walker's *Appeal* was published on September 28,
1829, and despite the fact that he knew his life was in
danger, he continued to urge the slaves to violently liberate
themselves. Even his own epitaph carried a message of
profound discontent for slavery; it also places the
burdensome consequence of slavery on the shoulders of
America:

*If any wish to plunge me into the wretched
incapacity of a slave, or murder me for the truth,
know ye, that I am in the hand of God, and at your
disposal. I count my life not dear unto me, but I am
ready to be offered at any moment. For what is the
use of living, when in fact I am dead. But
remember, Americans, that as miserable, wretched,
degraded and abject as you have made us in
preceding, and in this generation, to support you and
your families, that some of you whites on the
continent of America, will yet curse the day that you
were ever born. You want slaves and want us for
your slaves!!! My colour will yet root some of you
out of the very face of the earth!!!!*

David Walker mysteriously died, his death came a year
after his *Appeal*; nevertheless, he made his mark on
nationalist or revolutionary history as it related to the black
slave.

I'd be remiss if I didn't say that Walker's appeal was
partially in accord with the Declaration of Independence.
This in part was the justification for his call to blacks to

rise with force and militancy to destroy their white slave masters.

Bishop Henry McNeal Turner, another conscientious nationalist, made these impassioned statements:

*Are we men!! -- I ask you -- are we Men? Did our Creator make us to be slaves to dust and ashes like ourselves? Are they not dying worms as well as we... How we could be so submissive to a gang of men, whom we cannot tell whether they are as good as ourselves or not, I could never conceive.*

*...America is more our country than it is the whites -- we have enriched it with our blood and tears. The greatest riches in all America have arisen from our blood and tears; -- and will drive us from our property and homes, which we have earned with our blood?*

This *Appeal* was first considered as the most definitive position on the question of black assertiveness during and after slavery.

Bishop Henry McNeal Turner was, without doubt, the most prominent and profoundly vocal advocate of black nationalism via black emigration in the years between the Civil War and the First World War. By constant agitation he evoked and sustained African-American awareness of their African heritage and their disabilities in America.

It was, of course, America's diabolical treatment of black people that gave birth to Turner's all-consuming nationalism.  Turner believed a revolution was necessary, and it must take the form of emigration to Africa., He strongly believed that the only remuneration for the victims of white American nationalism would be black African nationalism.

Bishop Turner worked feverishly to elevate black people on a level of dignity and self-respect; however, he adamantly believed that this could only be achieved by way of emigration.

> *I do not believe any race will ever be respected, or ought to be respected, who do not show themselves capable of founding and manning a government of their own creation.*

Bishop Turner died in 1915, never witnessing his dream of African repatriation.  It was his influence and others that led to the great mass movement known as "Garveyism".

I shall briefly mention a couple of other nationalists before getting to the heart of my project.  These people were also Christian nationalists, who played a vital part in assisting our people along the path of racial p[ride and dignity.  The influence and/or impact on our struggle returns with the Garvey movement.  I shall discuss that aspect of my research following my discussion of the following nationalist:

Martin R. Delaney attempted to start his own back to Africa emigration movement.  His ideal colony would be somewhere in Nigeria.  He thought very little of Liberia, as he saw it as being a colony of white business interests.

Delaney and other Charleston blacks launched the Liberian Exodus Stock Steamship Company to provide for emigration to Africa. The company's *Azore*, made its first and only voyage because of inexperienced planning and incompetent operation by the ship's white captain, the company lost the *Azore* in debtors court.

An interesting point to make is that Delaney was responsible for Garvey's "Africa for the Africans" slogan.

Reverend Alexander Crummel, a pure African, educated by private charity at Queen's College, England -- where he became acquainted with President Roberts and others, and from whom he obtained such information of Liberia which determined him to make that country his permanent residence. He believed that all men should hold some relation to the land of their fathers. He didn't beckon African-Americans to Africa *en mass*, however, he did point to the inferiority of blacks as the reason for their scorn and lack of interest in Africa.

*Why talk to us of Fatherland? What have we to do with Africa? We are not Africans, we are Americans. You ask no peculiar interest on the part of Germans, Englishmen, the Scotch, the Irish, the Dutch, in the land of their fathers; why then do you ask it of us?*

*Alas for us, as a race! so deeply harmed have we been by oppression that we have lost the force of strong, native principles, and prime natural affections. Because exaggerated contempt has been poured upon us, we too become apt pupils in the school of scorn and contumely. Because repudiation*

*of the black man has been for centuries the wont of
civilized nations, black men themselves get shame at
their origin and shrink from the terms which indicate
it.*

Reverend Crummell had an ideological impact on
Bishop Turner; Turner heard an address by Alexander
Crummell, and shortly thereafter accepted his position on
African repatriation. Crummell urged black Americans to
analyze the rich resources of Africa, so that they could
assist in developing the land for the race's benefit. He also
appealed to Christian interests in Africa (missionary work)
which he felt would alleviate white influence. He raised an
extremely poignant question relating to emigration and
African resources: "How shall the children of Africa,
sojourning in foreign lands, avail themselves of the
treasures of this continent?"

He supplied a fairly tenable answer to the
aforementioned question; if individuals are unable to enter
upon a trading system, they can form associations. If one
has not sufficient capital, four or six united can make a
good beginning. If a few persons cannot make the venture,
then a company can be formed.

Despite the fact that Crummell supported colonization
on the ground that it would extend Christianity to so-called
"heathen" lands, he subsequently went to Africa in the
interest of Christianity and colonization.

He maintained a loyal allegiance to Christianity;
nevertheless, his contributions to African racial pride and
African patriotism is highly commendable. Crummell's
nationalism came at a later period in his life. In addition

to Henry Turner, Marcus Garvey was also influenced by Crummell's plea for repatriation.

Furthermore, Crummell's observation and open admission that the African had a deep yearning for a higher religion, only gave the African's sense of Islam as a logically pristine religious structure more depth, creditability, and understanding. Despite his desire to Christianize Africa, he acknowledged the fact that Islam was rapidly and peacefully spreading to the tribes of Western Africa, even to the Christian settlements of Liberia.

It is interesting to note, that, Crummell and Edward Wilmot Blyden were close associates. Blyden could very well have been influential in getting Crummell to see the revolutionary potency that Islam offered the African. Blyden, one of the early Pan-African patriots, not only advocated emigration to Africa, but also believed that Islam was far more advantageous to the African personality than Christianity. This he objectively voiced despite his allegiance to Christianity.

Edward Wilmot Blyden, was one of the first Pan-African nationalists who embraced the tenets of Islam. Although he did not, according to most historical evidence, become a practicing Muslim, he never relented from his vociferous advocacy of Islam for the Africans. In this respect, it might be safe to say that he was one of the first advocates of black Muslim nationalism.

Blyden published fifteen of his articles and essays under the title, "Christianity, Islam and the Negro Race." One of these articles was written for the *Methodist Quarterly*

*Review* on "Mohammedanism in West Africa." After two expeditions into the interior of Sierra Leone, he wrote "Mohammedanism and the Negro Race." Blyden never ceased to laud the Muslims for their ban on alcoholic drinks, their devotion to learning, and the stimulus they gave to artisan crafts and trade.

He seemed convinced that it was the African convert to Mohammedanism and the Negro colonist from Christian countries, who did more for the permanent advance of civilization in equatorial Africa. He believed that Mohammedanism- by its simple, rigid forms of worship, by its literature, its policies, its organized society, its industrial and commercial activities - was rapidly superseding a hoary and pernicious paganism.

Blyden constantly attacked Christianity for having imposed racial inequalities upon black people and felt that the absence of pictorial representation in Islamic societies had saved black people from having great and holy people always depicted to them as white. This absence had great advantage for the African convert to Islam. His Arab teacher having no pictures by which to aid his instruction, was obliged to confine him to the book. In this way, his thinking and reasoning powers were developed rather by what he read and heard than by what he saw. He saw neither busts nor pictures, but men. He did not study books, but characters. And among the first lessons he learned was, that a man of his own race, Bilal Ibn Rabah, an African, assisted at the birth of the religion he was invited to accept. And, in subsequent training, his imagination never for one moment endowed the great men of whom he heard or read with physical attributes essentially different from his own.

There is no doubt that Blyden's philosophy contributed greatly to the historical roots of African nationalism, Pan-African and Negritude, and have been a source of inspiration and pride to modern advocates of African nationalism. In addition to others, Blyden should be considered one of the greatest fore-runners of Pan-Africanism and African Islamism to date. Blyden's racial, nationalistic, and Islamic philosophy, directly or indirectly, influenced Marcus Garvey, Noble Drew Ali, Elijah Muhammad, and George Padmore. It might also be safe to say that Blyden enhanced Duse Muhammad Ali's Islamic nationalism.

Duse Muhammad Ali, one of Africa's more fervent African nationalists, was born of an Egyptian father and a Sudanese mother in Alexandria, Egypt, November 21, 1866. Duse's study and love of history prompted him to found his famous and influential journal *The African Times and Orient Review*, which began publication in July 1912, the same year that Edward Wilmot Blyden died. In addition to this publication, nationalist activities, and anti-colonial policies, he also advocated higher education in Africa. He felt that what was needed most was a thoroughly equipped University in Africa whose degrees would be recognized by the Universities of England. This idea had been voiced earlier by Edward Blyden.

Duse's residence in England was an extremely active one; however, the one factor which enhances his stature as an African nationalist was his crucial influence in awakening the students in England to the importance of African history. He generated among them that vital nationalist feeling of "looking back to past greatness."

Duse worked very hard to show the past achievements of the African ancestors.

His profound affection and erudition of African history led to his election to membership in the Negro Society for Historical Research and later on to the American Negro Academy. His emphasis on African history instilled pride in the African students of that period.

History attests to the fact that Duse's ideas and personality had a profound impact on the philosophy and organizational policies of Marcus Garvey. Garvey's early political involvement in Jamaica, and his uncompromising racial views prompted him to go to London in 1912. While in London he was in contact with many African Students and workers, finally, he became associated with Duse and *The African Times and Orient Review.*

Garvey was an astute student of Duse and a tireless worker for the journal. He absorbed much knowledge about history, geography, Islam, and Africa's mineral resources. It is understandable that Duse's ideas would have a magnetic attraction and effect on Garvey, considering the fact, that Duse's remarks and activities in behalf of the African was always in full focus.

Garvey's slogan, "African for the Africans, at home and abroad" was indicative of the race pride, and dignity he received from Duse. In 1918 Garvey began a newspaper in New York, called the *Negro World* on which Duse later worked during his stay in the United States.

Duse Muhammad was constantly propagating and/or promulgating Islam from all perspective levels. He was actively involved with the Muslim community in Africa, particularly, Lagos Nigeria. In England, he became associated with Muhammad Ali and Khwaja Kamal al-Din of the Working Mosque; he was frequently in the company of the English convert to Islam, Muhammad Marmaduke Pickthall, whose work titled *The Glorious Quran* won wide acclaim.

Also, he was associated with Lord Healy, and especially with the noted scholar Abdullah Yusuf Ali, who completed one of the best English translations of and commentaries on the Holy Quran. While in London, he organized and founded the Indian Muslim Soldiers Widows and Orphans War Fund; he also served as vice-president of the London-based central Islamic Society. During his residency in The United States, he founded the Universal Islamic Society in Detroit.

Another extremely important feature of Duse's life was the profound influence he and his belief in Islam had on Marcus Garvey. Consider the Garveyite motto "One God, one aim, one destiny," the one God aspect being akin to the Islamic emphasis on the oneness of God or God's unity.

Many pioneer Garveyites still discuss with emphasis the fact that "Garvey was taught by a Muslim" and many say that he at times referred to Islam as the black man's religion. Consider the Garveyite hymn for their President, which reflects an Islamic tendency in the first stanza:

*Father of all creation*
*Allah Omnipotent,*
*Supreme O'er every nation*
*God bless our President.*[29]

Despite the fact that Duse Muhammad Ali was a fervent nationalist, he was not, in the strict sense of the word, a racist. Although many of his enunciations were shrouded in racial overtones, he was never classed as an enemy of the Caucasian race. He was an intellectual "race man" who believed strongly in the religion of Islam.

He devoted his life to the reconstruction of the economic, moral, and cultural life of people of African descent.

Duse Muhammad Ali like Blyden before him contributed much to the platform of black nationalism via Islamic tenets.

Duse died June 25, 1945.

The reader is encouraged to read Duse Muhammad's prolific and historical account of modern Egypt: *In the Land of the Pharaohs.*

---

[29] Amy Jacques Garvey, Garvey and Garveyism, (Kingston, Jamaica, 1962), pp. 176.

# Garveyism and Islam

The Ahmadiyya movement was another vehicle that gave the black man an outlet for positive self expression. The Ahmadiyya movement originated in India in 1889 as a Muslim reform movement. It has grave differences with orthodox Islam in that Hazrat Mirza Ghulam Ahmad (1835-1908) was the so-called promised Messiah. For this so-called un-orthodox position, they have been ostracized from the broader Islamic community. Nevertheless, it has, since its inception, developed the most aggressive missionary program in Islam. They have also done some prolific work in Africa.

The Ahmadiyya's came to the United States in 1921 and settled in Chicago. Its founder, or Imam Dr. Mufti Muhammad Sadiq, began to publish a periodical, *Muslim Sunrise*. An interesting point to note is that many of its converts consisted of blacks. This can be attributed in part to Islam's basic message of human equality. A large number of these blacks were Garveyites. Consider the year 1923, a year of intense proselytizing by Dr. Sadiq, a year that also enabled him to meet many Garveyites at a liberty hall meeting.

The contact among members of the Garvey movement and the Ahmadiyya's remained a close one. Interestingly, Dr. Sadiq successfully managed to convert over forty Garveyites to Islam before returning to India in 1923.[30]

---

[30] <u>Race First</u>, Tony Martin, Greenwood Press, Westport, Connecticut, 1976, pp. 73-76.

According to Dr. Tony Martin in his academically informative book titled *Race First*, the Garvey movement at its 1922, convention proposed that the movement adopt Islam as its official religion. The reason was that three-quarters of the black world was Muslim and Muslims were better Christians than Christians. Garvey did not legislate on this proposal.

Dr. Martin also informs us that some Negro world writers went so far as to compare Garvey with Prophet Muhammad.

In a paean of praise entitled "Sing of Garvey", "Glorify him, ye Myriad Men of Sable Hue," referred to him as "Child of Allah." Even the organization's Universal Ethiopian hymn, compiled by Rabbi Arnold J. Ford (a leader of Harlem's so-called Black Jews) contained a hymn "Allah-Hu-Akbar" based on African lyrics.[31]

The Ahmadiyya Muslims did not succeed in building up a mass movement primarily because of the strong Christian influence among blacks, and Garvey's reluctance to legislate on Islam. Nevertheless, the Islamic influence on such men as Noble Drew Ali and Elijah Muhammad came by way of the Garvey movement.

Noble Drew Ali, founder in 1913 of the Moorish American Science Temples, acknowledged Garvey's influence on his movement. Interestingly, Drew had for his movement a major theological document, a Holy Quran

---

[31] Ibid., pp. 77.

compounded of the teachings of the bible, Marcus Garvey, and the Quran.

It has been suggested that the Honorable Elijah Muhammad was a corporal in the ranks of the Chicago UNIA division. Some people say they remember him as an active member of the Detroit UNIA. It has been established, however, that Muhammad did some of his early converting in Chicago in 1933 in UNIA Liberty Hall. Furthermore, he constantly referred to his movement as the culmination of the Garvey movement.

The Moorish-Americans and the Nation of Islam were successful at attracting a substantial number of Garvey's followers.

The Moorish Americans were fairly successful at attracting Garvey's followers after his deportation. Some of Garvey's followers considered Noble Drew Ali to be Garvey's rightful successor. On the other hand, there were some Garveyites who were extremely alarmed and angry at this organizational exodus. As a result, the Philadelphia Garveyites wrote the United States authorities in 1935 and asked that Garvey be returned for the purpose of combating this loss of membership problem.

The Moors continuously stressed to their converts that their movement came from the authority of Marcus Garvey, and they denounced orthodox Garveyites as rabble rousers and crooks, who had deviated from the path of Garveyism.

Interestingly, despite the Islamic influences in the UNIA and the Islamic influences on Garvey by way of Duse

Muhammad Ali and Edward Wilmot Blyden, these influences did not impel Garvey to take a position on religion. On the contrary, he remained neutral on the issue of religion. According to Dr. Tony Martin, the essence of religion for Garvey was the imparting of race pride, Black nationalism, and self reliance. In this light, his willingness to tolerate Islam and the attraction he had for Muslims is not difficult to understand.

Every group of a black nationalist persuasion was welcomed into Garvey's UNIA. The Black Jews of Harlem and the Black Christian Nationalists could find a home in the UNIA, for the basic thrust of their doctrines was essentially the same message of race pride and self-reliance. Garvey was concerned only with primary essentials; the issue of religious nationalism came after Garvey was no longer on the scene. The concept of religious nationalism was ushered in by Noble Drew Ali(Timothy Drew).

Before I discuss Noble Drew Ali, let me briefly discuss the methodology that Garvey, Ali, and Elijah Muhammad utilized in structuring their organizations. There are three philosophical terms that these men employed, that I am sure will aid us in appreciating their genius:

(1) The eclectic approach, choosing what appears to be the best from sources, systems, and styles.

(2) The synthesizing approach, the combining of separate elements of substances to form a coherent whole.

(3) The holistic approach, emphasizing the importance of the whole and the interdependence of its parts.

Garvey was an astute student of history, and having such a quality enabled him to carefully study his predecessors.

Garvey selected the concept "Race First" from a brilliant African-West Indian by the name of Hubert Harrison. The concept of African repatriation was selected from Martin R. Delaney (The so-called father of black nationalism). Garvey's idea for an independent shipping company, such as the Black Star Line, came from Paul Cuffee and Captain Harry Dean. The slogan "One God, One Aim, One Destiny," was selected from Duse Muhammad Ali; furthermore, the concept, or slogan "Africa for the Africans," and the glorification of African history was extracted from the black nationalist teachings of Edward Wilmot Blyden and Duse Muhammad Ali.

The idea for an independent school system, and independent economy, and Garvey's sense of leadership mission was triggered by reading "Up from Slavery," the autobiography of Booker T. Washington. These major concepts and slogans, among others, were synthesized into a unique movement called the United Negro Improvement Association (UNIA). The organizational framework of the UNIA was based on these various concepts and slogans.

Moreover, Timothy Drew (Noble Drew Ali) not only extracted most of the main tenets of Garveyism, but incorporated the religion of Islam as well. This radical act made Drew Ali the first religious nationalist in the United States.

Another point that must be made is that although Garvey was aloof from religious matters, he saw a dire need to dismantle the caucasian image of God and Jesus. Garvey pointed out that a white God cannot be The God of black people; this was the God of the white man. The black man's God must be black. Of course this concept was continued by Drew Ali and Elijah Muhammad.

Drew Ali sought the religio-psychological release from a vicious white dominated society; on the other hand, Garvey sought release by way of removing blacks to an independent African state. Drew Ali utilized Garvey's psychological glorification of Africa, by telling his followers that they were descendants of the Moors from Morocco in North Africa.

His followers would be called Asiatics - this philosophy, in addition to the African nationalist concepts of Garvey, was in effect a psychological antidote to the presence of white christian America. The problem of white racism was being addressed by giving black people a knowledge of Africa, and by giving them a new identity. Garvey, by way of selecting and synthesizing the African pioneers teaching into a compact wholeness, was able to pave the way for Drew Ali. Drew Ali by way of employing the same methods was able to pave the way for the Honorable Elijah Muhammad.

An important point to make is that some contemporary African-American historians stubbornly refuse to concede to the fact that it was Islam that elevated Africa to new heights of glory after the historical or cultural demise of Egypt, and Southern Africa. The reason for refusing to openly acknowledge that fact may be based on the belief that Islam is non-African. Another reason or rational may be the association of Islamic Arabs with African slavery.

Historical facts and acknowledgements even from Caucasians who have professed to be dire racists have stated that Islam was and is a force that gave Africans an indomitable will and spirit. A well-renown professor and racist of the 1920's made the following statements:

> *Concerning Islam's steady progress in black Africa there can be no doubt. Every candid European observer tells the same story. "Mohammedanism", says Sir Charles Elliott, "can still give the natives a motive for animosity against Europeans and a unity of which they are otherwise incapable." T. R. Threlfall wrote: "Mohammedanism is making marvelous progress in the interior of Africa. It is crushing paganism out. Against it, the Christian propaganda is a myth. ... The rapid spread of militant Mohammedanism among the savage tribes to the north of the equator is a serious factor in the fight for racial supremacy in Africa. With very few exceptions the colored races of Africa are pre-eminently fighters. To them the law of the stronger is supreme; they have been conquered, and in turn they conquered. To them the fierce, warlike spirit inherent in Mohammedanism is infinitely more attractive than is the gentle, peace-loving, high moral standards of Christianity; hence, the rapid headway the former is making in central Africa, and the certainty that it will soon spread to the south of the Zambezi.*[32]

---

[32] The Rising Tide of Color Against White World Supremacy, Lothrop Stoddart (New York, Charles Scribner's Sons, 1920), pp. 94 & 95.

Obviously his thesis and other notes he used placed the African and people of African descent in a subhuman category; namely, because he was emotionally and academically appealing to various racist groups that were mainly involved in anti-African activity. These groups' primary concern was the justification of European colonialism in Asia and Africa. They were also anti-East European immigration.

His contention was that until the white world proved itself capable of organizing and maintaining organization strength, the threat of black and brown attack was a constant possibility. Islam was the main factor that threatened white rule in Asia and especially in Africa. He makes the following comments:

> *Insofar as he is Christianized, the negro's savage instincts will be restrained and he will be disposed to acquiesce in white tutelage. In-so-far as he is Islamized, the negro's warlike propensities will be inflamed, and he will be used as a tool of Arab Pan-Islamism seeking to drive the white man from Africa and make the continent its very own.*[33]

He continues by saying that Islam is a militant religion by nature, and once it is embraced by the African, it can become a dangerous weapon of liberation.

> *Pan-Islamism once possessed of the Dark Continent and fired by militant zealots, might forge*

---

[33] Ibid., 96 & 97.

*black Africa into a sword of wrath, the executor of sinister adventures.*[34]

If racist whites could acknowledge the power of Islam in Africa, when will so-called enlightened black historians do the same? The serious historian should remember this very significant quotation:

*No historian can take part with -- or against -- the forces he has to study. To him even the extinction of the human race should merely be a fact to be grouped with other statistics.*

Lothrop Stoddard graduated from the Harvard Law School in 1908, but he practiced law for less than a year. He returned to Harvard where he received the M.A. degree in 1910 and the Ph.D. in 1914. His doctoral thesis was the study of the revolt of the Negroes against the French colonists in San Domingo in the late eighteenth and early nineteenth centuries, in which large numbers of white colonists were killed and a Negro state was set up.

Stoddard's central theme was that the white races -- particularly the so-called Nordics -- were in danger of being inundated by the "inferior" races who had a much higher birthrate.

---

[34] Ibid., 102.

# The Nation of Islam: Apex of Religious Nationalism

By the late 1920's, the UNIA and the Moorish Science Temples were shorn of their aggressive, charismatic leadership. Suffice it to say, these organizations gave the black masses some degree of hope; they reminded blacks of their human worth as a people, and their proud African heritage. Needless to say, the heinous result of racist oppression continued to take its toll on the minds of black people. It was this deplorable condition that gave rise to another messianic leader of black people -- one Wallace D. Fard. Fard maintained the synthetic, eclectic, and holistic methods of Garvey and Drew Ali. However, Fard's psychology was far more encompassing insofar as race pride, and the dismantling of white godly supremacy were concerned.

Fard taught in a language that was highly esoteric and appealing to the lost masses. Expressions such as: "The black man is the original man," "The white man is the devil," found literal meaning in the hearts and minds of many former Garveyites and Moors.

Fard managed to seize on Moorish and Garveyite passions and transformed them into a new dynamic force, in which religious, economic, racial, and political energies were fused.

Fard's chief convert, Elijah Muhammad, was wise enough to see similarities between Garveyism and Drew Ali's movement. He also regarded Fard as the highest missionary for black people. Fard's approach to the black problem was based on the need to extricate black people from white Christianity, and white idol worship.

Garvey and Drew Ali tried to turn the black man away from the white man's god. Garvey by way of saying that the messiah was black; Drew Ali was saying that Islam was the black man's true religion.

Fard synthesized these two positions and raised them to the highest level. After the disappearance of Fard, Elijah Muhammad became the uncontested leader of the Nation of Islam.

Elijah Muhammad channeled all his energies towards achieving the aims and aspirations of his downtrodden people. He proceeded by analyzing the concepts and philosophies of past black leaders. Needless to say, that Garvey and Drew Ali had the greatest impression on him.

Drew Ali's movement was a kind of religious separatism, the thrust of Garvey's UNIA was the political economy of separatism. Elijah Muhammad like his predecessors before him utilized the synthetic and the holistic approach in reconciling these two philosophies.

Elijah combined religion, economics, politics, racial, and social ingredients to accomplish his basic aims and objectives. Unlike Marcus Garvey and Drew Ali, Elijah recognized the relationship between economic self-sufficiency and socio-political power. The fusion of these various philosophical elements is what made the nation of Islam the apex of black nationalism.

Elijah patterned the character of his organization after Garvey and Drew Ali.   Like Garvey and Ali, he was committed to racial uplift and to the unification of black people.    Like Drew Ali, his racial philosophy was subordinate to Islamic catechisms.   He found an inner security organization which he called the Fruit of Islam; this was also patterned after Garvey's Order of Nobility.

Like Drew Ali, Elijah stated with far more reaching enhancement that the black man was the original man, the Asiatic blackman, the maker, the owner, and the cream of the planet Earth.   This kind of racial doctrine was the culmination of a racial identity for black people.

Elijah also knew that for a people to amount to anything, it is necessary to have a nationality and a land. "North America", he said, "is only an extension of the continent of Africa."

As I stated earlier, Noble Drew Ali gave his followers Morocco as the seat of their nation.   But he realized that the dark people of the world are also native to the continent of North America, which was and is under European domination.   Therefore, the Moors stressed obedience and loyalty to the flag of the United States, so long as they were living in America.

Unlike Nobel Drew Ali, Elijah Muhammad was not a man who would compromise.  He preached separation from the socio-economic, and political authority of white people. Employing a more pragmatic approach, he stated that the black people now inhabiting the Western Hemisphere should strive to build here in the wilderness of North

America a nation of Islam, wherein we will enjoy freedom, fraternity, justice, and equality.

This kind of teaching stirred the masses to such an extent that the construction of independent schools, the purchase of farmland, and international commerce came into being.

There are some who say that the death of Elijah Muhammad brought about the death of the Nation of Islam. There are some who say that the nationalistic teachings of this movement had served its purpose; therefore, there was a need for a religious teaching that embraced all of humanity.

On the other hand, there are some who say that as long as black people are oppressed there is a need for a movement such as the Nation of Islam. The schism that exists between Minister Louis Farrakhan and Imam Warith Deen Muhammad is predicated on the two above positions.

Philosophical and religious contentions have existed among the black Muslims ever since their birth. After the disappearance of Fard, a group of black Muslims who had been in the Moorish Science Temple confronted Elijah about the term Asiatics. They wanted to continue to be known as Moors (Moroccans).

Another splinter group under the leadership of one Abdul Muhammad wanted to be known as Ethiopians and they also adopted the principles of Marcus Garvey as their creed or philosophy. Of course there were other doctrinal disputes over the years, but none which merits serious attention.

The next serious dispute came between Malcolm X and his mentor and teacher, Elijah Muhammad. This dispute was historically significant in that it set a precedence that struck at the very fabric of so-called orthodox Islam and Islamic nationalism. This precedence has resulted in the disputatious division between blacks who are Muslims (so-called orthodox), as opposed to blacks who are black Muslim nationalists.

Viewing it from another perspective, one could say that the split we now see between Muhammad and Farrakhan is not a split between two Muslims, but a disputatious carryover between the staunch black Muslim nationalist leader, Elijah, and the newly transformed orthodox Islamic internationalist, Malcolm.

Interestingly, it has been stated and written that Imam Warith Muhammad was inspired by Malcolm in the direction of Islamic orthodoxy. However, careful research indicates just the opposite. In the *Autobiography of Malcolm X*, Malcolm on one occasion in particular, stated how much regard he had for Wallace's (Warith) spiritual opinions. He also stated that it was Wallace (Warith) who encouraged him to study Islam more in depth.

Malcolm's transformation to so-called orthodox Islam is an issue that has been written about and philosophically discussed for years. It is not necessary to continue this discussion at this time. However, there is a chapter in the appendix which I devote to Malcolm.

The point must be made that Imam Muhammad took the Nation of Islam on a path that reflected his spiritual character and his spiritual experiences. He was never a devoted teacher of nationalism of any kind; therefore, his approach to the Nation of Islam should be understood within the context of his spiritual experiences.

On the other hand, Malcolm's so-called transformation was not -- I believe -- a total religious transformation, but one I consider to have been based on expediency. It has been viewed as a means of reaching a wider black audience than the one the nation had provided. Malcolm having gone to the East in 1959 saw the same "blue-eyed White Muslims" then that he saw when he made the hajj. His interest was centered around an attempt to meet requirements for a coalition with major black civil rights organizations that were preaching establishment politics and integration.

Suffice it to say, that despite Malcolm's so-called orthodox Islamic transformation, he did not appreciably alter his black consciousness preachments.

Moreover, I hope that new material will be written about Louis Farrakhan vis-a-vis Malcolm in the near future. Questions should be raised such as: Does Farrakhan see himself as a reflection of Malcolm X? Similar to Malcolm, does he view himself as a demagogue? Is he on a similar international path as Malcolm? And is the scriptural division between Imam Muhammad and Farrakhan so vast that it cannot be reconciled? One thing is certain: Farrakhan commands a large black following that nourishes itself on black consciousness teaching -- Nation of Islam style.

Also, there is a considerable number of black people, Muslim and non-Muslim, who simply believe that Imam

Muhammad has not proven himself as a creditable leader. He received everything of noted worth when he succeeded his father; the temples which he later transformed into masjids, schools, a newspaper, businesses which he closed for various reasons, farmland, and a following that accepted him because they did not want to contribute to disunity, and the chaos it would bring by not accepting him. Of course, there were those who accepted him for his religious sincerity.

Furthermore, Imam Muhammad has not been credited, as his father has been, for transforming drug addicts, reforming prostitutes, enlightening the illiterate to the point of pursuing scholarly endeavors, and consistently speaking in defense, or on behalf of the black masses.

Similar to Warith Deen Muhammad, Farrakhan also encouraged his followers to register to vote.  Farrakhan believed that black people's vote for Jesse Jackson would be a demonstration of unity, but if white America failed black people, it would prove to black people that we are not a part of the inner fabric of the American system.

Similar to Warith Deen Muhammad, Farrakhan has, up to a point, failed to discuss alternative politics -- socialism, a labor party, and more importantly, an independent black labor party. More significantly, they, to my knowledge, have not consistently met with progressive black intellectuals to map a strategy for a black political agenda.

Farrakhan seems somewhat removed from consistently discussing power-politics -- he evaluates issues primarily in a religious or scriptural sense -- or from the standpoint of black and white confrontations.

In a speech in Washington, D.C., Farrakhan stated that he did not understand why some black politicians did not support Jesse Jackson for President, which indicated to me that he did not fully understand power-politics and the unusual alliances it can and does produce.

On the contrary, Malcolm knew and understood the dynamics of power-politics. He subsequently began to seriously study capitalism, imperialism, and their political alternatives -- socialism.

Malcolm also attacked the Democratic and Republican parties as being the parties of corruption, exploitation, and racial oppression around the world.

Moreover, Farrakhan's support of Jesse Jackson and other black politicians is one thing, but the dynamics of American international politics (monopoly capitalism) is another.

Therefore, it is imperative that Minister Farrakhan assess the world situation as it relates to Islam, and how American capitalism and Russian imperialist socialism are the primary antagonists to Islam and third-world independence.

I should hope that a more in-depth research project is undertaken in the near future with regard to the history of Islam in America in general, and the birth of the Nation of Islam in particular. A biographical history of Elijah Muhammad is most needed if one is to fully understand the essence of the Nation of Islam. Also, a biographical history of Imam Warith Muhammad is needed if one is to fully understand his religious positions. Furthermore, a historical and philosophical study should be done on the ideological dispute between Warith Deen Muhammad and Louis Farrakhan. Placing these issues in proper perspective might permit us as a captive people to overcome our captivity. I say that because the Nation of Islam had a profound effect on the lives of black people from all walks of life. And, more importantly, it clandestinely shaped and set in motion various kinds of political and economic decisions that affected black people. Similarly, Imam Warith Deen Muhammad is affecting a new generation of black people who refuse to view their problems as African-Americans in racial terms.

Like the rebellious Muslim slaves before them, the Nation of Islam was regarded by the black masses as the catalytic agent for change in America. Will the black masses be receptive to this rebirth of the Nation of Islam under the direction of Minister Farrakhan? Will the black masses accept the humanistic teaching of Imam Warith Deen Muhammad and only involve themselves in black consciousness (nationalism) teaching from a rational, non-emotional point of view? Undoubtedly these questions along with others deserve serious study.

Imam Warith Deen Muhammad's American Muslim Mission (formerly The Nation of Islam) should be appreciably analyzed within the context of the black struggle. The American Muslim Mission under the leadership of Imam Muhammad has embarked on a path of human growth and development that is unparalleled in the history of Islam in America. Imam Muhammad believes that as long as the struggle of African-Americans is based on black consciousness teaching, the human quality of

African-Americans becomes the prisoner of black consciousness teaching. He makes the following point in his highly informative book *As The Light Shineth From The East*:

*If you keep calling yourself black, pretty soon you see yourself in blackness and not in humanness.*

This position has merit when one considers the fact that initially the nationalist or race teaching of Drew Ali, Marcus Garvey, and Elijah Muhammad was designed to transform an inferior people to functional worth; however, this teaching took on a new and different dimension in the 1960's and early 1970's, and subsequently became a license for a lot of despicable acts that had blackness at the forefront.

Blackness by philosophical definition was never clearly elaborated on; therefore, the narrowness of the term did damage after its validity declined. Dancing black, singing black, talking black, and looking black (Afro), and dressing black (dashiki) became the criterion for black acceptance.

Maintaining and emphasizing the need for black people to think mathematically, scientifically, and to strive for spiritual, and moral excellence got lost in the rhetoric of black consciousness teaching.

Rationally speaking, we must accept the fact that white racism was responsible for black nationalist teaching; furthermore, we must acknowledge that this race teaching did serve a purpose for a people who were made to look upon themselves as subhuman. However, it is very important to note that to dwell on the external factors of the human being and not on the internal qualities will almost always cause a person to lose contact with the human spirit.

"I am black and I am proud," and "black is beautiful" says nothing about the individual who is making such statements. "I am black and I am proud" is an utterance that is made to psychologically satisfy a need for acceptance into the human family on an equal basis.

It is imperative that I inform the reader that I am respectful of black nationalism and Pan-Africanism because of their ability to heal the sickness of inferiority; however, when anything is taken in excess it tends to make one ill again.

*(Since the initial writing of this book, the American Muslim Mission has become the Muslim Mission. Imam Muhammad removed all restrictive labels, thereby placing the movement in a universal context.)*

I must say that I am equally respectful of the courage, the determination, and the religious foresight that Imam Warith Deen Muhammad has displayed. Despite the fact that I disagree with him on some vital points, he presents a challenge to black nationalists, Pan-Africanists, Marxists, and people of various religious, and political persuasions in America and throughout the world.

However, this challenge must take place in the intellectual arena, and not on the physical battlefield.

From what I have seen Minister Farrakhan is not only continuing to teach the importance of being proud of being of African descent, but also the importance of moral, spiritual, and character development. In that regard he and Imam Muhammad are in somewhat agreement.

In the early days of the Nation of Islam the emphasis was on moral, spiritual, and character development by way of self-knowledge, self-awareness, self-sacrifice and self-discipline. As the Nation became popular, particularly during the 60's and 70's the concept of blackness, black power, and materialism began to reign supreme. As a result, respect for human dignity, lawfulness, and character development declined drastically.

Additionally, there were those who lived accordingly because the "Messenger" said that they should, and by adhering to the belief that "by nature black people were righteous."

This particular teaching or concept permeated the hearts and minds of those who accepted it to the extent that they became obsessed with living righteously, and severely criticizing those whom they felt were not. When Imam Muhammad changed, or modified the very teaching or concept that pumped life into their veins, chaos and subsequent spiritual death overtook many of them. However, for others that enforced teaching prepared them to be better Muslims in the traditional sense of the word.

I sincerely hope that a serious balance can be reached between the importance and need for race pride teaching, and moral and spiritual refinement. My hope was raised when a meeting between Minister Farrakhan and Imam Muhammad took place on August of 1983, and on two other occasions.

The meeting between Imam Muhammad and Minister Farrakhan occurred on August 11, 1983, and it stated the following:

*Both of us have a real interest in protecting the image of Muslims and keeping that image of Muslims in a favorable light.*

It was also stated that because of their mutual love for Islam and for the maintenance of peace between their communities, both agreed to future meetings. Another interesting point that came out of this meeting was the offer by Imam Muhammad to sell the properties that were purchased by the Honorable Elijah Muhammad to Minister Farrakhan, or the Nation of Islam. These properties consisted of a school and temple on Stony Island Avenue in Chicago, Illinois.

It is most unfortunate that within a year after this historic meeting, the followers of Imam Muhammad voted not to sell the above mentioned properties to Minister Farrakhan. The reason(s) was not publicly given. Furthermore, Imam Muhammad levelled very strong criticisms against Minister Farrakhan for allegedly referring to Judaism as a dirty religion, and for allegedly threatening the lives of an African-American news reporter and his family. These criticisms were levelled at the height of Farrakhan's support for Jesse Jackson for President.

Seemingly, Muhammad would have conferred with Farrakhan pertaining to the accuracy of these allegations. By not doing so, Imam Muhammad broke the verbal agreement between him and Farrakhan, and furthered the schism within the African-American Muslim community.

The African-American Muslim community, in my judgment, has the ability to revitalize Islam throughout the world. African-Americans are Muslims by choice, as opposed to most third-world people, who are Muslims by tradition. That unique fact alone places African-Americans in a unique position to be vanguards for a renewed Islamic spirit.

That is why men such as Farrakhan and Muhammad, considering their influence among African-Americans, should dispense with the unnecessary doctrinal arguments. In my estimation, an individual is a Muslim as long as he or she believes in the oneness of God, and all of his prophets from Ibrahim to Muhammad (Peace Be Upon Them). That belief should suffice for us to work together to try to bring about a meaningful change in a society that groups all Muslims and African-Americans together anyway.

No one can deny the spiritual purity of Islam, nor can any objective student deny that Islam was introduced to every country in accord with its socio-economic, political, and cultural ramifications.

Every Islamic country in the third-world believes in and practices the fundamental tenets of Islam; however, every country applies its own cultural standards, or rather incorporates its culture standards into Islam.

The Mandingoes cultural practice of Islam is different from the Arabs, the Chinese is different from the East Indians, and so on.

Despite these factors, Islam remains a flexible, spiritual, and political phenomena in the world. Islam stands on its own spiritual and historical merit. There is no need for anyone to defend or rescue Islam from so-called heretics.

It appears that Minister Farrakhan is modifying, and fusing the teachings of the Honorable Elijah Muhammad with certain Islamic principles of humanitarian concerns; if this analysis is correct, then other meetings between Muslims can serve as a broad base coalition for Muslims, African-Americans, and right minded people in general.

Furthermore, Farrakhan's support of minority people in particular and oppressed people in general, places him in a favorable position as a spokesman for impoverished African-Americans and third world people.

Similarly, Imam Muhammad's appeal to people of conscience affords him a position of spiritual reformer, and moral crusader.

It is important for the reader to know that Elijah Muhammad stated on many occasions that he was not teaching Islam according to tradition, but according to the condition of black Americans. He fully understood some of the Arabs' anger over the methods he employed to uplift black people racially and religiously; he asked that they understand, and he further stated that one day traditional Islam would be taught to his followers.

Despite the contention in the African American community as to whether or not Imam Muhammad is an accomplished leader or organizer, he has without a doubt proven to be an Islamic scholar par-excellence. His

Islamic writings and teachings could very easily compete with the best of Islamic scholarship and erudition.

Another important issue that needs to be considered is that it behooves the followers or sympathizers of Imam Muhammad to stop criticizing Farrakhan as a hypocrite because he decided after three years of following and supporting Imam Muhammad that he could no longer, in what Farrakhan calls good conscience, do so. The importance of this issue continues in that the accusation, or charge of hypocrisy has also been levelled at Imam Muhammad for following and supporting his father, and waiting until his father's death to fiercely denounce him and his method of introducing Black Americans to Islam. Needless to say, both accusations are pointless.

It should be mentioned that Farrakhan, to date, has not written any books that speak to the spiritual, academic, and moral needs of black people. Also, to date, he has not opened any schools on a national, or in many instances, on local levels. He has not, to the best of my knowledge, purchased any farmland, nor does he have a viable business (excluding the possibilities of P.O.W.E.R.). His primary interest has been the lecture circuit.

I think it is imperative that Farrakhan by way of his eloquence, and by way of the pen, address the areas of Christian and Islamic theology; also, global politics as they relate to people of color, domestic political economy, and the caste-class practices among African Americans.

Not long ago, the Nation of Islam had been scripturally asserting that the Honorable Elijah Muhammad was not physically dead. Bernard Cushmeer (Jabril Muhammad), a writer, and minister, has written several articles which have been compiled in book form titled *Is it Possible That The Honorable Elijah Muhammad is Still Physically Alive?* has gone to great length to rationalize that (Nation of Islam) assertion by way of Biblical and Quranic verses that equate the Honorable Elijah Muhammad's presumed death with that of the presumed death of Jesus on the cross.

According to the Gospels, and there are fourteen points in the Gospels, that state that Jesus did not die on the cross, but died a natural death: Cushmeer utilizes these points as well as Quranic and other sources to state the following:

> *Upon close examination, as you can see, if you took the few minutes to read these fourteen points, the New Testament revolves around whether or not Jesus really died when they said he did. Or you may agree with Mr. Ali that he did not die at that time at all. Read, think, draw your own conclusions as to whether or not you think whoever is written about died there on the cross or not. Be objective. Try to determine whether or not the words there in the Bible really teach of a death or of a narrow escape.*

> *Now, consider this: If the Bible's Jesus is really a future Jesus, just what are we being told? I know that many Muslim scholars think what is taught of Jesus refers to the history of Muhammad 1,400 years ago. I have read their comparisons. They miss the mark by a wide margin. They often try to bend or twist prophecy to fit various parts of Muhammad's history. This is not to say that certain prophecies were not partly fulfilled in his history. In these*

*instances he serves as signs of events fulfilled in the life of Master Fard Muhammad, His Messenger, and us.*

*Mr. Ali refers to Maulana Muhammad Ali's research on the New Testament's treatment of Jesus and his death.    Maulana Muhammad Ali also translated the Qur'an into English.*

I believe that some people still believe strongly in the Honorable Elijah Muhammad and accept and need the idea that he is still physically alive and will sit on the right side of Allah when Allah is ready to pass final judgment on the 20th Century Babylon (The United States).    As I stated earlier, the death of Elijah Muhammad actually killed the hope, the spirit and destiny of many of his followers.

It is unfortunate that many of his followers believed more in the "Messenger" than they did in the actual tenets of Islamic theology.    They lived Islam for the "Messenger," not for themselves on the basis that Islam is a way of life for the Believer.    As a result, when Muhammad physically left their presence, many of his followers fell from spiritual grace -- gone was the radiant glow from their faces, the pride in self, the external cleanliness, the overly mannerable disposition, and the fanaticism to live righteously.

Some say that it wasn't until Farrakhan returned to the fold that new life was restored in those who lost it.    If this is true, then Farrakhan has served a useful purpose.

Does the concept of the risen, or resurrected Christ, and Elijah's escape from death -- which means he could not have risen, since risen, or resurrected means to return to life after death, belong to Farrakhan's spiritual evolution as he calls it, or does it belong to Bernard Cushmere (Jabril Muhammad)? I would think that Cushmere believes in it more so than Farrakhan since he is the one who postulated it.

These questions and the contradictions surrounding them must be immediately resolved for people who need a better understanding.

Around 1982, Farrakhan indicated that Elijah Muhammad had escaped a death plot during the time that he was ill in the hospital. This death plot information, according to Farrakhan, was exposed by a Caucasian prostitute, who was at a party and overheard high government officials discussing it. She in turn informed her black pimp of what she heard, and he in turn informed Farrakhan. The time factor was never mentioned, nor was the subject pursued.

Believe it or not, what is important to know is that Elijah Muhammad never referred to himself as the Christ, nor did he ever say that he would be resurrected. In fact, he taught against life after death.

He referred to his teacher Master Fard Muhammad as the "Savior", and "Allah in personage". He referred to himself as the "Messenger of Allah" to Black people a little later in his mission. He used various aliases before he took on this title of "Messenger."

There is no doubt that Master Fard Muhammad was Elijah's "Savior," but Elijah was Malcolm, Farrakhan, and the Black masses' "Savior". Considering the above information, some very important questions come to my mind. For example: how long did Farrakhan know about the so-called death plot? Did he know about it during, or immediately after his break with Imam Muhammad? If so, why did he wait so long to share it with the Black community? When did he come into his spiritual awareness that the Honorable Elijah Muhammad is the resurrected Christ? Why did it have to take Bernard Cushmere (Jabril Muhammad) to quicken Farrakhan back to spiritual life, and back into Elijah Muhammad's fold?

The cooperation of African American Muslims, I believe, can only bring about positive changes in a society where people are yearning for character development, racial pride, human dignity, spiritual, and moral rejuvenation. As I said earlier, the teachings of race pride and self-sufficiency is not a racist act providing it is done within the context of a historical, sociological, and psychological perspective. Moreover, those African American Muslims who ignore the fact that we are constantly confronted with American racism by criticizing those African-American Muslims who have decided to confront that racism in a forceful manner as not living up to the tenets of Al-Islam are in my mind, very historically ignorant.

These issues and constructive criticisms are by no means designed to berate anyone's Islamic veracity, but are raised because a lot of people are wondering where the African American Muslim community is going. Many people looked at the Garvey Movement and the old Nation of Islam as a light of hope for the suffering masses. On the contrary, many people don't think Farrakhan could organize Black people to an appreciable degree. Also, many think people that Imam Muhammad is too compromising with the American system.

My position is clearly based on history. African Americans need more than one voice that speaks to their needs, wants and aspirations. We have always had religious leaders and political leaders who are usually the religious leaders as well as race leaders. In other words, there is a need for Imam Muhammad and Farrakhan regardless of what I, or anyone else thinks.

My intention for raising these issues is for the sake of mental exercise and logical argumentation. If I have offended anyone, I offer my humble apology.

I also believe that the contributions that were made to the social, moral, economic, and intellectual development of African-Americans by the Honorable Elijah Muhammad must remain on the pages of history.

The Nation of Islam under the sagacious leadership of Elijah Muhammad brought Islam to African-Americans as a viable alternative religion; he taught the importance of adopting Arabic names, of reading and studying the Holy Quran, and he heightened our awareness of Prophet Muhammad (PBUH!) These factors cannot and should not be obliterated from the pages of history.

Those African-Americans who profess to believe in orthodox Islam must honestly admit that their conversion, directly or indirectly, came by way of the Nation of Islam. Historians, philosophers, Islamic scholars and the like must, systematically, place the teachings of Elijah

Muhammad in proper perspective. Historical and psychological explanations must be given as to why he taught such fierce religious nationalism. This is a task that awaits serious, objective minded scholars.

Finally, the political, economic, and moral situation in the United States and in the world demands that people of conscience come together. This demand excludes their religious, social, racial, economic and political persuasion, for the purpose of making the world safe for future human development, and harmonious human interaction.

# The Decline of Islam in Brazil

The Portuguese were the first Europeans to sense the importance of the African slave trade. Although they utilized Indian slavery to the maximum extent throughout the sixteenth century, they introduced Africans into Brazil as early as 1538; that is when the first shipment of Africans from the Guinea coast reached Bahia. Actually, it was the introduction of sugar into the colony around 1540 that activated interest in and importation of African slaves; after that time the slave trade continued unabated. It was during the period of Spanish control, 1580-1640, that the slave trade to Brazil increased at an enormous rate.

It is interesting to note that prior to 1441 the Portuguese had not indicated a preference for African slaves. Any non-Christian they could obtain was fine, and even Christian slaves could be found in that country as late as the sixteenth century. The Portuguese expansion in Morocco was stifled after their defeat at Algiers in 1437. As a result, a steady supply of Muslims never really developed. Indeed, a moral argument justifying the enslavement of Muslims had not been necessary. It was simply a war against Al-Islam, and to the Portuguese, that was a war against evil. Hence, that was an innately noble activity.

Moreover, the slavery of white Christians was a long-time tradition in Iberia and, although the Catholic church gradually adopted an intransigently hostile position toward it, the practice continued. It adjudged a phenomenon involving unfortunate individuals rather than races, and if an individual succeeded in emancipating himself, he could become a full-fledged member of society. This idea of accepting emancipated slaves was one of the extenuating features of Brazilian slavery.

Additionally, there was no law prohibiting slaves to read and write; in many instances, they were taught to the point that many of them became proficient in the use of the Portuguese language. There was a law requiring that slaves be baptized within at least one year after their arrival into the country. In keeping with this baptism, slaves were expected to attend mass and confession on a regular basis. By doing this, the church was in effect saying that the slaves had souls. This actually placed the African slaves in a position that was rarely, if ever, enjoyed in the English colonies. Furthermore, the manumission of slaves was encouraged in Brazil.

These paradoxical social forces in Brazil produced a dual situation for Muslim slaves. First, they managed to enjoy a relatively uninterrupted religious structure; second, and these are two factors combined in one, they became the most ardent slave insurrectionists in Brazil; and, because of social and cultural variables, they lost their Islamic roots. I will briefly discuss the first aspect, then make the necessary transition to the second.

Just before Islam became extinct in Brazil, such men as Nino Rodrigues, Etienne Brasil, and Manoel Querino were able to observe and study it. Their description of the Islamic community in Brazil was as follows:

> *It was essentially a Puritan community. Its outward morality, sobriety, and temperance contrasted strongly with the other Africans' noisy*

*exuberance and their liking for alcohol and for singing and shouting. The Moslems' appearance, their quiet conversational tone, restrained gestures, and pointed beards symbolized their ethnic and religious separateness. Above all, the Moslems's faith set the rhythm of his life, marking its every phase, from birth to death, accenting the passage of the day from sunrise to sunset.*

*It appears that a Mussulman baby was baptized at birth. By the time he was ten, he had been circumcised. Then his instruction would begin, for the Mohammedans attached great importance to education. Since his faith required the reading of the Koran, he had to be able to read and write Arabic script. Schools were, therefore, established in conjunction with the Moslem places of worship, in the homes of free Africans. House searches conducted after Hausa or Mina revolts produced alphabets, reading primers, and wall posters of lessons to be learned. In Rio, Arabic grammar [books] written in French were used. Free members of the community even went to Africa to study so that they might later devote themselves to teaching the slave population of Brazil.*

Despite this obviously religious tolerance and the accepted traditions of the slaves, the over-all treatment of them was not good enough -- especially for the Muslims. Muslim insurrections broke out in Brazil in 1756, 1757, and 1772. Five times, from 1807 to 1835, Muslims in Bahia revolted against what their religion did not accept scripturally -- slavery of body and of mind.

Before I continue elaborating on the slave revolts, I must share with you the prevailing disposition of the Muslims that was, in most instances, the catalyst for the revolts. According to Gilberto Preyre, historian, Islam flourished and branched out in Brazil in the form of a powerful sect that prospered in the dark of the slave huts, and with teachers and preachers from Africa to give instructions in reading the books of the Quran in Arabic, and with Mohammedan schools and houses of prayer functioning there.

He continues by stating the following:

> *The atmosphere that preceded the movement of 1835 in Bahia was one of intense religious ardor among the slaves. In Mata-Porcos Lane, on the Praca slope, at St. Francis-Crops, in the very shadow of the Catholic churches and monasteries and the niches of the Virgin Mary and St. Anthony of Lisbon, slaves who were schooled in the Quran preached the religion of the Prophet, setting it over against the religion of Christ that was followed by their white masters, up above in the big houses. They propagandized against the Catholic mass saying that it was the same as worshipping a stick of wood; and to the Christian rosary with its cross of our Lord, they imposed their own, which was fifty centimeters long, with ninety-nine wooden beads and with a ball in place of a crucifix on the end.*

An interesting point to make at this juncture is that, anti-catholic prejudices among Muslims influenced other Africans and Mestizos to be biased toward Protestantism. Preyre conveys more relevant information pertaining to the cultural impact of the Muslim slaves on Brazilian dress among the women, and their remembrance of their religious practices.     Religious remembrances was manifested by way of long prayers, fasting, no alcohol, sacrifices of sheep, and vestments consisting of long white tunics.

Obviously, it was the pristine tenets or Al-Islam that motivated and galvanized these Muslims in their insurrectionary activities. Suffice it to say, that these were not just mere slave revolts, these Muslims resented their status as slaves; more importantly, they had immense pride in their Islamic heritage. They, therefore, believed that they were engaging in a holy war (jihad) against the infidel. In their masjids and in their secret societies, they plotted against other Africans who would not join them as well as the slave masters for whom they harbored a fierce hatred. In 1807, 1809, 1813, and 1816 there were outbreaks in Bahia. In 1813, for example, the Muslims arose one morning at four o'clock, burned the homes of their slave masters as well as their own slave quarters. They died rather than surrender. In January 1835, the officials heard of plans of a great uprising. Every precaution, including a search of the slaves quarters, was taken in order to prevent the uprising. At one place the searching officials were fired on and were overcome. The uprising continued to such an extent that the entire city of Bahia was completely terrified.

The best testimonial to the bravery and courage of the captured Muslim leaders is the fact that instead of being hanged as common criminals they were shot with full military honors.

I would be historically negligent by not pointing out that two to three hundred years before insurrections in Brazil, Muslim were fiercely agitating for their freedom in the Americas.

In Santo Domingo in 1522, Muslim rebellions touched off a review of royal policy, and the conclusion was that a combination of Muslim gelofes, meaning that they were from Senegal or Sierra Leone, and disgruntled Ladinos, Christianized african slaves who spoke spanish or had some knowledge of spanish culture, had been responsible for the frightening challenge to white authority.

Consequently, there were decrees on February 25, 1530 and on September 13, 1532 that specifically prohibited the dispatch of any Muslim, Ladino or Jewish slaves into the Americas. As a matter of fact, King Fernando the Catholic issued the first document in 1501 concerning the importation of Muslim slaves into the Americas. The idea was to stop Al-Islam from coming into the Americas because Muslims were known to influence the other slaves.

Fernando gave instructions to Sir Nicolas Ovando, the appointed Governor of the Indies. He enjoined him, "Not to allow to enter into the colonies any Muslims, but to permit to come other African slaves with the condition that they be born under Christian power." It is not enough for me to discuss the Muslim slaves and accompanying social forces, I am compelled to briefly mention that there were Muslims who continued to have contact with Africa. Freyre suggest that during the early part of the nineteenth century, many Fulahs and Mandingoes served as traders between Bahia and the West coast of Africa.

These men of commerce brought such items as kola nuts, cowry shells, cloth and soap from the West coast and palm oil to Brazil. Many of these Muslim slaves returned to West Africa after they got manumitted, or escaped, Professor Michael Turner of the City University of New York wrote in his *Os Prestos no Africa: Brazilian Slaves in Dahomey* (a paper presented at the graduate student conference on the continent of Africa that the Muslim slaves that returned to Dahomey following the slave trade in Brazil, built the first masjids in the capital. These Muslims were always seen by the Portuguese as the aristocrats of the Senzalas (slave quarters). They came from a society with advanced political and literary cultures and because of this, including the Islamic and Quranic injunctions, they saw their enslavement by the Portuguese who were of lesser cultural and religious sophistication as utterly demeaning. This feeling of self-importance, and knowing that they were only slaves to Allah, instilled in them the uncontrollable determination to destroy the slave system.

The decline and subsequent extinction of Al-Islam in Brazil until recently has a sociological explanation.
Muslims in Brazil were always a minority of the population. After the revolt of 1813, they were diminished considerably, either by firing squad or by deportation. As a result, those who remained made few if any converts, Roger Bastide, an anthropologist, believed that it was the religious, and in some cases, tribal snobbery that impelled them to remain aloof from the non-Islamic Africans.

Additionally, Islam in Brazil represented "Puritanism", primarily because of its prohibition of excessive drinking, which was particularly hard on wretched slaves seeking an escape from reality in the sugar cane brandy known as "cachaca".[35]    To the slaves, the Muslims were not comrades in slavery, they were only comrades in insurrectionary situations. This, of course, made the few Muslims left in Brazil vulnerable to impending social and religious dynamics.

The reader should bear in mind that Portuguese authority, based on the historical prevalence of the Spanish decrees, and the physical and financial hardships involved in controlling Muslim slaves, were more interested in paganized Africans for their slave colony. The idea behind this view was that the non-Muslim slaves were usually more obedient and more apt to become submissive Christians.

Hence, as the Muslims came into contact with pagan Africans in Brazil, as their slave revolts failed and their numbers declined, they in turn became more conciliatory to their environment. In essence, they were absorbed by pagan cults. It must be said that in West Africa, Al-Islam has, for the most part, triumphed over fetishism or paganism. It drove it back and gained a firm hold on the African continent. It even opposed Christianity vigorously, and in many instances, was successful. But, in Brazil, it only enjoyed brief moments of cultural victory.

---

[35] The African Religions of Brazil, The John Hopkins University Press, (Baltimore & London, 1978), pp. 146, 153, & 154.

Bastide puts it very succinctly and poignantly when he said that in differing demographic and social conditions, the collision of races and cultures can produce the most surprising happenings and the most contradictory religious metamorphoses.

I would be remiss if I did not indicate that Al-Islam has returned to Brazil. The largest assemblage of Muslims appeared on August 26, 1975 for the purpose of attending the inaugural ceremony of the then King Faisal Masjid which is considered to be the second grand masjid in South America. This masjid was built with Saudi Arabian donations. There are, based on my last research project, nine masjids in Brazil, and the Egyptian Ministry of Religious Affairs had posted four Imams at the following cities: Curitiba; Sao Paulo; Barretos; and Paranagua.

Presently, there are some 600,000 or more Muslims of Arab descent in Brazil, and they are mostly concentrated in Sao Paulo -- the largest city in Brazil. In light of this information, it is, therefore, imperative that concerted efforts be made to establish Islamic centers under the control of leadership of devout and reasonably zealous Islamic workers in Brazil and throughout South America. Such a unique undertaking would most certainly lead to the revival of Al-Islam, not only in Brazil, but also in those South American countries where Muslims are experiencing the problem of an acute shortage of religious teachers and imams.

# Muhammedu Sesei of Gambia & Trinidad, 1788-1838

Muhammedu Sesei was a Mandingo African who was another victim of the Trans-Atlantic slave trade, but who managed to return to Africa. He too belonged to a small minority of literate ex-slaves who either had the opportunity of writing a diary or journal, or of relating the main events of his life to an interested European. Captain John Washington, according to Carl Campbell, received the main source of information about Sesei. The Mandingoes in Port of Spain, Trinidad, were diligently trying under the leadership of Jonas Muhammed Bath to get repatriated to Africa; unfortunately, they failed as a group, but Sesei did manage to return to his native land of Gambia.

Muhammedu Sesei was born about 1788 or 1790 of parents who were Muslim Mandingoes. According to historical records he did not die in 1838. This was the year when, having reached Gambia, he disappeared from historical records.

In that year he was about 48 or 50 years old, and he had passed about half of his life in Africa and half in the West Indies. Sesei was born in Nyani-Maru, a village on the north bend of the river Gambia, about 100 miles upstream. In the West Indies he had spent most of his time in Trinidad.

A very relevant point must be made here and that is that Captain John Washington was primarily interested in the accounts of Sesei because of British imperialist concerns.

Many British traders were concerned with the commercial significance of Gambia, and the importance of British domination of Gambia and upper Senegambia. The reader must bear in mind that Britain and France were rivals in the quest for African land.

Captain Washington intended to get from Sesei as much information about the interior of Africa as his brain could yield. Washington, Secretary of the Royal Geographical Society, was also interested in African languages, and the geography of Africa.

Washington was very much aware that Africans like Sesei who had been exposed to British influence for about a quarter of a century in the West Indies could be very useful in breaking the hostility of some Africans to British commercial penetration of the African hinterland.

As a member of the 3rd West India regiment, Sesei was "Kingsman", distinguished from the slave. Interestingly, Sesei never experienced plantation slavery, immediately after his capture he was impelled to join the regiment.

Sesei and other Africans fought in the wars of the King of England, mostly against the French. Sesei saw active service against the French in Guadeloupe; he was stationed in Barbados.

In 1825 Sesei's regiment was demolished, and he was discharged with good conduct. The disbanded soldiers from this regiment and the 6th Regiment were given lands on the east coast of Trinidad away from the slaves on the west coast plantations. The British government undertook to spend money on these settlements up to the amount of the pensions of all the men settled there.  Sesei was to spend most of his life in the West Indies.

Historical records show that Sesei did not receive land nor pension -- the reason why is unknown.  He quickly moved to Port of Spain, and subsequently became a member of the Muslim Mandingo group led by Jonas Muhammed Bath.  As stated earlier, Bath was a remarkable man, and a very devout Muslim.  He was the leader of a Muslim Mandingo community that prospered economically, and on many occasions petitioned the British government to repatriate them back to Africa.

Of course the British government refused to honor this petition, and as a result, the Mandingoes had to settle permanently in Trinidad.  Sesei, however, refused to accept this turn of events; he was obsessed with returning to Africa.  This obsession prompted him to borrow 144 dollars from another Mandingo; he brought a passage for himself, his wife, and young child to England, where he arrived about the middle of 1838.

After landing in England, Sesei without enough money to maintain himself and family appealed to England for his pension and a passage to Sierra Leone.  As a result of this appeal, he fell under the protection of one Captain John Washington.  Washington took his case to the Colonial Office, which gave Sesei a small allowance and deliberated about how they could use his services.

Sesei was used to translate the Mandingo language.  He corroborated the existence of certain places on the Royal Geographical Society's map, and he told Washington of other sites not on the Society's map.

Washington, on an expedition to Gambia, employed Sesei as an interpreter, his intention was to foster trade with the Muslim Mandingo merchants of the Senegambia region.

Sesei agreed for a passage back home to escort any British expedition that desired to go into the interior of Gambia, or Senegambia.

The historical records indicate that from those expeditions there is every possibility that Muhammedu Sesei, alias Felix Ditt, did get back to the place of his birth.

John Washington's description of Muhammadu Sesei is as follows: "he is very intelligent, quick of wit, a devout follower of Islam. He knew the Quran verbatim; and he always carried certain verse of the Quran around with him."

He spoke "Negro English", and he wrote Mandingo indifferently in Arabic character. Sesei always displayed intelligence that was usually associated with the Muslim Mandingo community.

Some research on African descendants in Trinidad suggest that the facial features of Mandingoes on the island were very similar to Indians in India. Washington's description of Sesei substantiates this point of research.

Washington reported that Sesei's complexion and character of face resembled the Hindus or blacks of India. Washington's description of Sesei further stated the following: His features are regular and open, his person well formed, full six feet in height; his nose Roman, his nostrils rather flattened, not thick lips, beautiful teeth, hair wooly, colour, a good clear black, but not jet.

Washington was so impressed with Sesei that he encouraged William Carpenter, a London artist, to paint the portrait of Muhammadu Sesei.

The reader should study Captain John Washington, "Some Account of Mohammadu Sesei, a Mandingo of Nyani-Maru on the Gambia," Journal of the Royal Geographical Society, Vol. VIII (1838) pp. 448-454. Bulletin No. 7, December 1974, *African Studies Association of the West Indies.*

# Epilogue

In December of 1982, after what I thought was the conclusion of this project in January 1982, I was fortunate to go to Liberia, West Africa; I stayed there for four months and two weeks. During that time I was in constant contact with the Mandingo Muslim community; the Mandingoes are an isolated group of people who, for the most part, are traders and merchants. They believe strongly in Islam and adhere to most of its traditional tenets.

The Mandingoes are a nomadic people, who become citizens of a particular country by marrying that country's indigenous women. These women are almost never Islamic in belief, they are tribal in belief, and very often convert to Christianity.

Interestingly, I did not see too many converted Muslim women. The reason, I was told, was that they were still inclined toward their tribal habits and beliefs.

As I stated earlier, the Mandingoes are predisposed to traditional Islam coupled with the traditional African concept of what a woman's status should be. This might have had some unconscious effect on how the women viewed Islam vis-a-vis Christianity.

Muslims in Liberia, aware that they are surrounded by Christians, and several different tribes that practice African traditional religions, are content to remain in their communities, and to increase their economic status by way of trading, and engaging in various kinds of merchant operations.

The Mandingoes lived in small to large compact settlements. A primary level of stability within the Mandingo community was the family; the family was an extended one, whose members traded and farmed land. The senior man in the village arbitrated internal disputes and represented the group in the lineage or ward council. The stability of the Mandingoes was reinforced by the patrilineal and by virilocal rules of residence. A man's strongest social identity -- before his conversion to Islam -- seems to have been that of his lineage.

There are two other important points I would like to make pertaining to the Mandingoes. They and the Lebanese lived in the same community; they set up their businesses in the same community, but they did not worship together.

The reason I was given was that the Mandingoes pray differently from the Lebanese. This so-called reason was based on sheer frivolity, the Mandingoes are too Islamically traditional despite their African tribal leanings. In my mind, the Lebanese refused to pray with the Mandingoes because of cultural and ethnic biases. The Lebanese could not adequately explain to me what this difference in prayer performance was based on.

I explained to them, and they accepted, that a Muslim is one who submits to allah, and minor differences in prayers does not, and should not, make a difference in the worship of Allah.

Therefore, it became crystal clear to me that cultural and racial bias was the prevailing factor for separate prayer service. Another factor pertaining to this issue was the Lebanese Muslims refusal to close their shops at Jummah prayer service, and their complete disrespect for the total African community in which they resided.

As I observed all of these events, it became more apparent to me that the African-American Muslim will be the vanguard for change in the Islamic world.

I make this claim from the standpoint that the Muslim Mission, and to a certain extent, the Nation of Islam, are diligently trying to systematically and historically place Islamic traditionalism in its proper perspective.

The Muslim Mission, nor the Nation of Islam adhere to Sunni, Shia, Ahmadiya, or any other traditional sect. In this sense, that places them above and beyond the realm of traditional disputatious differences that exist in the Islamic world. More importantly, it enables them to see things as they relate to Islam more objectively.

A large percentage of the Mandingoes came to Liberia during and after the expansion of the Mali empire in the 14th Century. Mali came into existence after the Ghananian empire in 1236. Compared to the Ghananian empire before it, Mali was larger and wealthier. Unlike Ghana where traditional African religions were practiced, Islam predominated in Mali. Mali existed for two centuries.

After the death of its greatest emperor Mansa Musa who ruled from 1312 to 1336, the empire began to decline. Many of the people who left Mali after its decline were Mandingoes, Lormas, and Vais; these people migrated to Liberia, and other countries in that immediate region.

Not only in Liberia, and other parts of Africa, but particularly south of the Sahara, Muslims have to share their country with non-Muslims. Sometimes, as in Liberia, they are minorities and they resent the secularization brought in by Western Christianity which they feel is constantly trying to undermine Islam. The policy of Muslims in Liberia, and in Africa in general, is to maintain the essentials of their religion such as the rule of the Shari'a and their own educational system.

I also observed that through Islam, African-Arab solidarity was beginning to increase in Liberia. The Egyptian Muslim hierarchy sent emissaries to the Liberian Muslims for the purpose of assisting them in building more Islamic schools and Masajid (Mosques).

Moreover, Saudi Arabia is also a major contributor in Africa; as a result, Imams are converting large numbers of Africans. As I stated earlier, Africa is indeed the Muslim continent.

Additionally, it is imperative that the West come to terms that strategically speaking, three of the most important zones of Africa are Muslim held -- the Straight of Gilbrator on the Moroccan coastline, the Suez Canal-Red Sea region, and the Horn of Africa.

# Appendices

## A.  Islam and the African-American Convert

There is an on-going attempt by indigenous and immigrant Muslims to establish El-Hajj Malik el Shabazz (Malcolm X) as the pioneering advocate of orthodox Islam among African Americans.  They base their assertion on the fact that after Malcolm returned from hajj, renounced the Honorable Elijah Muhammad, and subsequently divorced himself from the Nation of Islam preachments, according to them, it was at that point that he embraced the pristine tenets of Al-Islam.  For them, this event unequivocally substantiates their claim.  They are correct insofar as it was Malcolm who set a popular precedent for orthodox Islam, but they are historically incorrect insofar as his being the pioneering forerunner of such a movement. This historically inexact view can easily be rectified if one would only search for the sources.  To quote Malcolm on this note, "History is best qualified to reward our research."  Let us now scrutinize the historical sources.

There were three documented attempts to institute orthodox Islam among African American.  There was the Institute of the Islamic Mission of America headed by Sheikh Al-Hajj Daoud Ahmed Faisal.  The Islamic Mission of America was established in Brooklyn, New York in 1928, and was incorporated in 1948 as a religious institution with full and complete religious, social and economic authority as required by the laws of the United States.  Sheikh Faisal was granted a charter by Sheikh Khalid of Jordan and King Saud of Saudi Arabia, which in essence reaffirmed his right to establish an Islamic mission in the United States. Within the period of time mentioned above, Sheikh Faisal purchased the Talbot Estate in East Fishkill, Dutchess County, in New York. This property was worth about half a million dollars and was purchased on a mortgage for less than a hundred thousand dollars. Furthermore, this property was, over a period of three years, converted into an expansive Muslim community; however, it was lost because of the lack of adequate finance. Sheikh Faisal taught his congregation that they were the children of Adam, the heirs and descendants of Ibrahim (Abraham), Ismail, Isaac, and Jacob. He tried to uplift African Americans with the spirit of the Qu'ran, the Sunnah of the Prophet and the Hadith, but African Americans were too steeped in the Christian doctrine to appreciate the crystal clear message of Al-Islam. Needless to say, Faisal only managed to attract a small number of followers. Equally important to note is that Sheikh Faisal is also credited with establishing the first Islamic school in America.

The second known attempt to convert African Americans to the creed of Al-Islam was made by a Sudanese named Muhammad Majid in 1927. He established the African Muslim Welfare Society of America (AMWSA). This organization was incorporated in 1928 as a religious body in Pittsburgh, Pennsylvania. According to research by Dr. Sulayman Nyang, this organization was mostly comprised of Arab Muslims, but it tried to recruit and proselytize African American in the Pittsburgh area. This noble effort was also thwarted because of African Americans' emotional attachment to Christianity, and, I believe, because of a lack of cultural understanding on the part of both parties.

A third attempt was made by Dr. Yusuf Khan of India, who sought to convert members of the semi-Islamic nationalistic movement, the Moorish Scientists of America. Paradoxically, it was these reformed Muslim nationalists who actually founded the first Muslim Masjid in Pittsburgh, Pennsylvania in 1930 for the propagation of the faith among African Americans.

Dr. Khan enlisted the support of Walter Bey, a former leader in the Moorish organization who usually taught Islamic principles in the absence of Khan. A point worth noting at this time is that a furor erupted within the Moorish community in Pittsburgh over the dramatic change in Islamic instruction. Of course, there were individuals who yearned for the unorthodox nationalist aspects of Islam, and there were individuals who learned to appreciate the orthodox aspects of Islam and the purity of the Holy Qu'ran.

As a consequence, verbal and sometimes physical confrontations erupted. However, time is the essence of all things; when the conflict subsided, the Muslims who wanted the faith in its pristine entirety remained with Dr. Khan and subsequently established the Masjid and an Islamic school. those who were adamant in their loyalty to the Moorish Science Temples continued with that school of thought, or they later embraced the teachings of the Nation of Islam.

Dr. Khan initiated some major religious reforms within the Moorish organization; these reforms would eventually compel its members to abandon their inclination toward nationalism entirely. Dr. Khan's primary reforms were:

*1. The use and recitation of the Holy Qu'ran*

*2. The use of Hadith;*

*3. The history of Prophet Muhammad (PBUH) as a source of spiritual guidance*

*4. Members were strongly encouraged to accept Arabic names.*

*5. He assisted in setting up an Islamic school which taught and stressed Islamic education, and conventional education.*

*6. The importance and significance of making salat.*

Within a short period of time, the believers were learning Arabic and the clear tenets of Islam at a rate that was highly impressive.

The irony or misgiving surrounding Dr. Khan's magnanimous deeds was the fact that he was an Ahmadis. The Ahmadis believe that Mirza Ghulam Ahmad is the promised messiah or mahdi. Ghulam claimed to be a prophet. This controversial subject produced another confrontation within the evolving community. Fortunately, this schism did not last long, but it did manage to sever the community once again.

Some members remained with the Ahmadis faction and contributed to its strength in another part of the city; while others, after property matters were legally resolved, engaged in the task of traditional propagation. Sayyid Ahmal assumed the leadership responsibility of disseminating Islam throughout the Pittsburgh area and the outlying regions after Khan left.

This Islamically conscious group was determined to maintain its faith despite much adversity and sometimes low group morale. Furthermore, these courageous efforts contributed, in small measure, to the evolutionary rise of Al-Islam among African Americans in that part of the country. For more information pertaining to this pioneering community, one should consult Jameela Hakim, who wrote a small book titled *Peace Amid Despair*. I think the best place to get exact information is in the Pittsburgh area.

Interestingly, and I am sure this will be unpleasant to some readers, the Ahmadis had an organized, consistent program or approach for the propagation of the faith among African Americans. The Ahmadis came to the United States from India around 1921, and settled in Chicago before branching outward. Their imam was Dr. Mufti Muhammad Sadiq. He began his proselytizing campaign in the Universal Negro Improvement Association (UNIA), the black nationalist organization headed by Marcus Garvey. Dr. Sadiq intensified his effort in 1923, the year that he met a number of Garveyites at a mass meeting. Afterwards, the social contact between members of the Garvey movement and the Ahmadis remained relatively close. Needless to say, the Ahmadis only managed to convert about forty or fifty Garveyites before Sadiq returned to India in 1923. Paradoxically, the Ahmadis did not succeed -- despite the close relationship between Garveyites and Ahmadis -- in building up a mass movement because of the deep sensitive connection of African Americans to Christianity. In fact, this particular situation insofar as Christianity and African Americans were concerned was the pivotal element in keeping African Americans away from Islam until the Nation of Islam emerged and gained popular and controversial attention.

Objectively speaking, I would be remiss it I did not point out that after Malcolm proclaimed his belief in Al-

Islam, it was Imam Warith Deen Muhammad who successfully placed the creed of the faith in proper perspective. He took members of the highly controversial and yet successful Nation of Islam away from the religio-nationalist posture that previously sustained its members. What must be pointed out in conjunction with the success of Imam Muhammad is that contrary to popular belief, the Honorable Elijah Muhammad actually paved the way for the adoption of orthodox Islam and the advent of Imam Muhammad.

What might be a surprising point to some readers is that Mr. Muhammad encouraged his followers to read the Holy Qu'ran, to study and emulate the life of Prophet Muhammad (PBUH) and live an exemplary life by applying the principles of Islam. In the early days of his leadership, he encouraged his followers to learn and practice making salat. He also taught the importance of learning the Arabic language, and he stressed the need for Islamic knowledge and Western education. He single-handedly revolutionized the quality and study of the Arabic language and the adoption of Islamic names. Consider the name Muhammad Ali which he bestowed on the former heavyweight champion, which in turn compelled some Arabs and others who had discarded their Islamic names for the purpose of assimilation to recapture their Islamic spirit and their

Islamic names.  Hence, no longer was Mahmud, Martin, or Abdul, Alfred.

On this same note, Dr. S. Muhammad Syeed addresses the manner in which the Nation of Islam employed the use of the English language to heighten the significance of Arabic.  He states: "One of the most striking features of the Black Muslims' English is the change in the spelling of the Arabic words already in use in English.  An attempt is made to spell the Arabic words in a way to represent their Arabic pronunciation as nearly as possible.  Thus "Muslim, Muhammad, and Qu'ran," which for centuries had been subjected to the nativization process of the English pronunciation and to the vagaries of spelling of English, were inconsistently spelled as "Moslem, Mohammed, Mahomet, Koran" and so on.  Syeed continues by noting that Black Muslim English "broadly identifies the direction of the development of Muslim English in America and may function as a common symbol of identity for Muslims in general."

I concur with Muslim journalist, Ghayth Nur Kashif, that the continuous rejection of the former Nation of Islam (Black Muslims) as a legitimate Islamic body has contributed, in large measure, to the failure to scrutinize the movement from a socio,psychological, and historical framework.

In conclusion, all of these individual and group efforts both orthodox and unorthodox have given birth to the phenomenal spread of Islam in America, particularly among African Americans;  therefore, none of these individuals or groups should be negated or obliterated.  As a result of these efforts, popular estimates of Muslims in

America range upwards to eight million; furthermore, an article by R. Max Kershar entitled "The Comparative Status of Christianity and Islam in the West," from *Newsweek* magazine (December 5, 1977) declared that the Muslim population had been increasing at a rate of 400 percent over the previous decade. According to present estimates, this phenomenal rate has not kept pace by direct conversion in recent years, but by inertia, birth rate and family ties, and the familiarization and acceptance of the Muslim community as a household factor in American life.

To reiterate, it might sound far fetched to some readers, but my continuous study of this phenomenon has led me to contend that it was not only the contributions of all the aforementioned groups and individuals, but especially the fierce religio-nationalism of Elijah Muhammad that ushered into existence the broad-based American acceptance of the Islamic religion as a viable creed for human growth and development. Muhammad Ali and Malcolm X were two members of that movement who contributed directly and indirectly to this unique situation.

## B. An Objective View of Malcolm X

Malcolm means many things to many people; in addition, many people have given the impression that they have captured the historical essence of Malcolm. Many books and articles have been written about him that almost always extol his revolutionary character. Orthodox Muslims, immigrants and indigenous, extol his Islamic -- Sunni Islamic assertiveness. Socialist declare that he made an overture to socialism once he renounced black nationalism for internationalism and subsequently discussed the ideological evil of capitalism verses the ideological goodness of socialism. I must say that I am somewhat annoyed by all of this. My annoyance is based on the fact that all of these themes continuously repeat themselves. Thus, Malcolm is only written about of discussed within the context of one's ideological persuasion.

There has not been a comprehensive book written that views Malcolm from a psycho-historical standpoint. Eugene Victor Wolfenstein attempted to write a psycho-social assessment utilizing Freudian and Marxian techniques in his *The Victims of Democracy*, but was derailed by his ideological and philosophical constraints.

I believe that an analytical approach to Malcolm's relationship with his parents and to the Nation of Islam -- especially to the Honorable Elijah Muhammad and his wife -- is essential to comprehending the morally reformed Malcolm and the subsequent Muslim revolutionary Malcolm. I also believe it is intellectually important to study other reasons why he divorced himself from the Nation of Islam. I surmise that two major reasons why he defected were his inability to resolve the issue of Muhammad's polygynous situation, and his impatience with the Nation of Islam's (NOI) passive posture regarding civil rights. Of course, his expulsion from the NOI (there is some evidence that it was contrived) heightened his internal agitation with the two above factors, but it also compelled him to re-evaluate himself within the realm of the black and third world liberation struggle.

An objective study of his relationship to his parents is extremely important considering the fact that his mother was a strong enduring woman who later suffered from a mental breakdown. She was also a woman who possessed a strong sense of racial and color consciousness. She was so obsessed with this aspect of her life that she often berated Malcolm about his light complexion. This display of complexion consciousness on her part resulted from shame of her mixed African ancestry. With regard to his father, Malcolm informed us that his father was physically brutal to his mother and brothers and sisters. However, he frequently showed partiality to Malcolm. Malcolm was usually exempt from physical punishment. I again surmise that this favored treatment by his father occurred because Malcolm was the proverbial seventh son, and because he was the lightest in complexion. Malcolm even alluded to this possibility in his autobiography.

Another extremely crucial point that I believe is critical for a better understanding of Malcolm was his on-going relationship with Imam Warith Deen Muhammad. Malcolm highly regarded Imam Muhammad's spiritual posture and his Islamic knowledge. How much of an impact he had on Malcolm's position regarding orthodox Islam has not been ascertained to any appreciable degree.

Bear in mind that Imam Muhammad took an adverse position to his father pertaining to orthodox Islam long before Malcolm.

It is pivotal to remember that Malcolm lost both of his parents at a very young age. He barely knew his father; therefore, the father-son relationship that Malcolm and Elijah shared was the crux of Malcolm's adult life. The ten year strength of this relationship was part of the foundation for Malcolm's greatness. However, the decline and termination of this father-son relationship abruptly compelled Malcolm to change directions whether he wanted to or not. He formed new alliances based on new needs and new objectives.

The turning point in his life did not arrive during or after he made hajj and acknowledged the existence of white complexioned Muslims. On the contrary, he always knew that there were white complexioned Muslims and European Muslims as well. He was taught that fact in the NOI; furthermore, he was frequently in the company of white complexioned Muslims whenever they visited the leader of NOI. And he most certainly saw and interacted with them when he was directed in 1959 to go to the east and make preparations for Mr. Muhammad to make umra.

Considering these facts, one should ask why did he loudly acknowledge something that he always knew? To answer this question, one must consider the time, various civil rights activities, and his uncontrollable eagerness to get involved in that struggle. I answer this question by extending my conjecture to include that he was seeking to ameliorate his relationship with civil rights leaders --

particularly Dr. Martin Luther King. He wanted to show them that he was no longer anti-white or anti-integration.

Moreover, upon careful scrutiny, one can see that the turning point for Malcolm started long before he made hajj. The hajj was the culmination of his spiritual transformation; on the other hand, his politics remained unchanged.

In conclusion, Malcolm must be studied and re-studied simply because he does mean many things to many people and because he epitomized so much of what the world is lacking today. He represented integrity, morality, courage, strength, ethics, and a dedication to progressive change. His autobiography -- which is in actuality a biography namely because Alex Haley continued writing it after his death -- should be reviewed with objective interest, and new themes should come forth about his religious, political, parental, social, and revolutionary life. Equally important, an objective approach to the impact of the Nation of Islam on Malcolm, and its contributions to the introduction of the Quran, Prophet Muhammad, and the Arabic language to African Americans must be properly assessed.

Most importantly, it must be pointed out that Malcolm's evolving character was not just an emotional or mechanical result of external causes. His external situation afforded him with the necessary materials for a subjective formative activity.

# Index

بِسْمِ اللَّهِ الرَّحْمَٰنِ الرَّحِيمِ

# PYRAMID BOOKS

"Books by & about people of African descent"

Celebrating 10 years: 1981 - 1991

This book is distributed by Pyramid Books, Inc., the first African-American owned and oriented chain of book stores in the United States. Founded by Hodari Abdul-Ali, Pyramid Books offers a large selection of books and related items "by and about people of African descent". To order copies of this book or to request our latest catalog, please write to:

## Pyramid Books, Inc.

PRINCE GEORGES PLAZA
3500 East-West Highway
Hyattsville, MD 20782
301-559-5200
Fax: 301-559-5202

Currently, in addition to our headquarter store in Prince Georges Plaza, we operate stores in the following locations:

THE HOUSE OF KNOWLEDGE
2849 Georgia Avenue, N.W.
Washington, D.C. 20001
202-328-0190

MONDAWMIN MALL
3062 Mondawmin Concourse
Baltimore, MD 21215
301-383-8800

HECHINGER MALL
1548 Benning Road, N.E.
Washington, D.C. 20002
202-396-1100

EUCLID PLAZA
220 Euclid Avenue
San Diego, CA 92114
619-266-8300

Writers' Inc. publishes literary works relevant to the spiritual, educational, economic and scientific development of individuals and communities. For additional information please write us:


Writers' Inc.
Post Office Box 746
Beltsville, Maryland 20705 USA